As We Go

Charles Dudley Warner

Contents

AS WE GO

BY

Charles Dudley Warner

OUR PRESIDENT

We are so much accustomed to kings and queens and other privileged persons of that sort in this world that it is only on reflection that we wonder how they became so. The mystery is not their continuance, but how did they get a start? We take little help from studying the bees --originally no one could have been born a queen. There must have been not only a selection, but an election, not by ballot, but by consent some way expressed, and the privileged persons got their positions because they were the strongest, or the wisest, or the most cunning. But the descendants of these privileged persons hold the same positions when they are neither strong, nor wise, nor very cunning. This also is a mystery. The persistence of privilege is an unexplained thing in human affairs, and the consent of mankind to be led in government and in fashion by those to whom none of the original conditions of leadership attach is a philosophical anomaly. How many of the living occupants of thrones, dukedoms, earldoms, and such high places are in position on their own merits, or would be put there by common consent? Referring their origin to some sort of an election, their continuance seems to rest simply on forbearance. Here in America we are trying a new experiment; we have adopted the principle of election, but we have supplemented it with the equally authoritative right of deposition. And it is interesting to see how it has worked for a hundred years, for it is human nature to like to be set up, but not to like to be set down. If in our elections we do not always get the best--perhaps few elections ever did--we at least do not perpetuate forever in privilege our mistakes or our good hits.

The celebration in New York, in 1889, of the inauguration of Washington was an instructive spectacle. How much of privilege had been gathered and perpetuated in a century? Was it not an occasion that emphasized our republican democracy? Two things were conspicuous. One was that we did not honor a family, or a dynasty, or a title, but a character; and the other was that we did not exalt any living man, but simply the office of President. It was a demonstration of the power of the people to create their own royalty, and then to put it aside when they have done with it. It was difficult to see how greater honors could have been paid to any man than were given to the President when he embarked at Elizabethport and advanced, through a harbor crowded with decorated vessels, to the great city, the wharves and roofs of which were black with human beings --a holiday city which shook with the tumult of the popular welcome. Wherever he went he drew the swarms in the streets as the moon draws the tide. Republican simplicity need not fear comparison with any royal pageant when the President was received at the Metropolitan, and, in a scene of beauty and opulence that might be the flowering of a thousand years instead of a century, stood upon the steps of the "dais" to greet the devoted Centennial Quadrille, which passed before him with the courageous five, 'Imperator, morituri te salutamus'. We had done it--we, the people; that was our royalty. Nobody had imposed it on us. It was not even selected out of four hundred. We had taken one of the common people and set him up there, creating for the moment also a sort of royal family and a court for a background, in a splendor just as imposing for the passing hour as an imperial spectacle. We like to show that we can do it, and we like to show also that we can undo it. For at the banquet, where the Elected ate his dinner, not only in the presence of, but with, representatives of all the people of all the States, looked down on by the acknowledged higher power in American life, there sat also with him two men who had lately been in his great position, the centre only a little while ago, as he was at the moment, of every eye in the republic, now only common citizens without a title, without any insignia of rank, able to transmit to posterity no family privilege. If our hearts swelled with pride that we could create something just as good as royalty, that the republic had as many men of distinguished appearance, as much beauty, and as much brilliance of display as any traditional government, we also felicitated ourselves that we could sweep it all away by a vote and reproduce it with new actors next day.

It must be confessed that it was a people's affair. If at any time there was any idea that it could be controlled only by those who represented names honored for a hundred years, or conspicuous by any social privilege, the idea was swamped in popular feeling. The names that had been elected a hundred years ago did not stay elected unless the present owners were able to distinguish themselves. There is nothing so to be coveted in a country as the perpetuity of honorable names, and the "centennial" showed that we are rich in those that have been honorably borne, but it also showed that the century has gathered no privilege that can count upon permanence.

But there is another aspect of the situation that is quite as serious and satisfactory. Now that the ladies of the present are coming to dress as ladies dressed a hundred years ago, we can make an adequate comparison of beauty. Heaven forbid that we should disparage the women of the Revolutionary period! They looked as well as they could under all the circumstances of a new country and the hardships of an early settlement. Some of them looked exceedingly well--there were beauties in those days as there were giants in Old Testament times. The portraits that have come down to us of some of them excite our admiration, and indeed we have a sort of tradition of the loveliness of the women of that remote period. The gallant men of the time exalted them. Yet it must be admitted by any one who witnessed the public and private gatherings of April, 1889, in New York, contributed to as they were by women from every State, and who is unprejudiced by family associations, that the women of America seem vastly improved in personal appearance since the days when George Washington was a lover: that is to say, the number of beautiful women is greater in proportion to the population, and their beauty and charm are not inferior to those which have been so much extolled in the Revolutionary time. There is no doubt that if George Washington could have been at the Metropolitan ball he would have acknowledged this, and that while he might have had misgivings about some of our political methods, he would have been more proud than ever to be still acknowledged the Father of his Country.

THE NEWSPAPER-MADE MAN

A fair correspondent--has the phrase an old-time sound?--thinks we should pay more attention to men. In a revolutionary time, when great questions are in issue, minor matters, which may nevertheless be very important, are apt to escape the consideration they deserve. We share our correspondent's interest in men, but must plead the pressure of circumstances. When there are so many Woman's Journals devoted to the wants and aspirations of women alone, it is perhaps time to think of having a Man's journal, which should try to keep his head above-water in the struggle for social supremacy. When almost every number of the leading periodicals has a paper about Woman--written probably by a woman --Woman Today, Woman Yesterday, Woman Tomorrow; when the inquiry is daily made in the press as to what is expected of woman, and the new requirements laid upon her by reason of her opportunities, her entrance into various occupations, her education--the impartial observer is likely to be confused, if he is not swept away by the rising tide of femininity in modern life.

But this very superiority of interest in the future of women is a warning to man to look about him, and see where in this tide he is going to land, if he will float or go ashore, and what will be his character and his position in the new social order. It will not do for him to sit on the stump of one of his prerogatives that woman has felled, and say with Brahma, "They reckon ill who leave me out," for in the day of the Subjection of Man it may be little consolation that he is left in.

It must be confessed that man has had a long inning. Perhaps it is true that he owed this to his physical strength, and that he will only keep it hereafter by intellectual superiority, by the dominance of mind. And how in this generation is he equipping himself for the future? He is the money-making animal. That is beyond dispute. Never before were there such business men as this generation can show--Napoleons of finance, Alexanders of adventure, Shakespeares of speculation, Porsons of accumulation. He is great in his field, but is he leaving the intellectual province to woman? Does he read as much as she does? Is he becoming anything but a newspaper-made person? Is his mind getting to be like the newspaper? Speaking generally of the mass of business men--and the mass are business men in this country--have they any habit of reading books? They have clubs, to be sure, but of what sort? With the exception of a conversation club here and there, and a literary club, more or less perfunctory, are they not mostly social clubs for comfort and idle lounging, many of them known, as other workmen are, by their "chips"? What sort of a book would a member make out of "Chips from my Workshop"? Do the young men, to any extent, join in Browning clubs and Shakespeare clubs and Dante clubs? Do they meet for the study of history, of authors, of literary periods, for reading, and discussing what they read? Do they in concert dig in the encyclopaedias, and write papers about the correlation of forces, and about Savonarola, and about the Three Kings? In fact, what sort of a hand would the Three Kings suggest to them? In the large cities the women's clubs, pursuing literature, art, languages, botany, history, geography, geology, mythology, are innumerable. And there is hardly a village in the land that has not from one to six clubs of young girls who meet once a week for some intellectual purpose. What are the young men of the villages and the cities doing meantime? How are they preparing to meet socially these young ladies who are cultivating their minds? Are they adapting themselves to the new conditions? Or are they counting, as they always have done, on the adaptability of women, on the facility with which the members of the bright sex can interest themselves in base-ball and the speed of horses and the chances of the "street"? Is it comfortable for the young man, when the talk is about the last notable book, or the philosophy of the popular poet or novelist, to feel that laughing eyes are sounding his ignorance?

Man is a noble creation, and he has fine and sturdy qualities which command the admiration of the other sex, but how will it be when that sex, by reason of superior acquirements, is able to look down on him intellectually? It used to be said that women are what men wish to have them, that they endeavored to be the kind of women who would win masculine admiration. How will it be if women have determined to make themselves what it pleases them to be, and to cultivate their powers in the expectation of pleasing men, if they indulge any such expectation, by their higher qualities only? This is not a fanciful possibility. It is one that young men will do well to ponder. It is easy to ridicule the literary and economic and historical societies, and the naive courage with which young women in them attack the gravest problems, and to say that they are only a passing fashion, like decorative art and a mode of dress. But a fashion is not to be underestimated; and when a fashion continues and spreads like this one, it is significant of a great change going on in society. And it is to be noticed that this fashion is accompanied by other phenomena as interesting. There is scarcely an occupation, once confined almost exclusively to men, in which women are not now conspicuous. Never before were there so many women who are superior musicians, performers themselves and organizers of musical societies; never before so many women who can draw well; never so many who are successful in literature, who write stories, translate, compile, and are acceptable workers in magazines and in publishing houses; and never before were so many women reading good books, and thinking about them, and talking about them, and trying to apply the lessons in them to the problems of their own lives, which are seen not to end with marriage. A great deal of this activity, crude much of it, is on the intellectual side, and must tell strongly by-and-by in the position of women. And the young men will take notice that it is the intellectual force that must dominate in life.

INTERESTING GIRLS

It seems hardly worth while to say that this would be a more interesting country if there were more interesting people in it. But the remark is worth consideration in a land where things are so much estimated by what they cost. It is a very expensive country, especially so in the matter of education, and one cannot but reflect whether the result is in proportion to the outlay. It costs a great many thousands of dollars and over four years of time to produce a really good base-ball player, and the time and money invested in the production of a society young woman are not less. No complaint is made of the cost of these schools of the higher education; the point is whether they produce interesting people. Of course all women are interesting. It has got pretty well noised about the world that American women are, on the whole, more interesting than any others. This statement is not made boastfully, but simply as a market quotation, as one might say. They are sought for; they rule high. They have a "way"; they know how to be fascinating, to be agreeable; they unite freedom of manner with modesty of behavior; they are apt to have beauty, and if they have not, they know how to make others think they have. Probably the Greek girls in their highest development under Phidias were never so attractive as the American girls of this period; and if we had a Phidias who could put their charms in marble, all the antique galleries would close up and go out of business.

But it must be understood that in regard to them, as to the dictionaries, it is necessary to "get the best." Not all women are equally interesting, and some of those on whom most educational money is lavished are the least so. It can be said broadly that everybody is interesting up to a certain point. There is no human being from whom the inquiring mind cannot learn something. It is so with women. Some are interesting for five minutes, some for ten, some for an hour; some are not exhausted in a whole day; and some (and this shows the signal leniency of Providence) are perennially entertaining, even in the presence of masculine stupidity. Of course the radical trouble of this world is that there are not more people who are interesting comrades, day in and day out, for a lifetime. It is greatly to the credit of American women that so many of them have this quality, and have developed it, unprotected, in free competition with all countries which have been pouring in women without the least duty laid upon their grace or beauty. We, have a tariff upon knowledge-- we try to shut out all of that by a duty on books; we have a tariff on piety and intelligence in a duty on clergymen; we try to exclude art by a levy on it; but we have never excluded the raw material of beauty, and the result is that we can successfully compete in the markets of the world.

This, however, is a digression. The reader wants to know what this quality of being interesting has to do with girls' schools. It is admitted that if one goes into a new place he estimates the agreeableness of it according to the number of people it contains with whom it is a pleasure to converse, who have either the ability to talk well or the intelligence to listen appreciatingly even if deceivingly, whose society has the beguiling charm that makes even natural scenery satisfactory. It is admitted also that in our day the burden of this end of life, making it agreeable, is mainly thrown upon women. Men make their business an excuse for not being entertaining, or the few who cultivate the mind (aside from the politicians, who always try to be winning) scarcely think it worth while to contribute anything to make society bright and engaging. Now if the girls' schools and colleges, technical and other, merely add to the number of people who have practical training and knowledge without personal charm, what becomes of social life? We are impressed with the excellence of the schools and colleges for women --impressed also with the co-educating institutions. There is no sight more inspiring than an assemblage of four or five hundred young women attacking literature, science, and all the arts. The grace and courage of the attack alone are worth all it costs. All the arts and science and literature are benefited, but one of the chief purposes that should be in view is unattained if the young women are not made more interesting, both to themselves and to others. Ability to earn an independent living may be conceded to be important, health is indispensable, and beauty of face and form are desirable; knowledge is priceless, and unselfish amiability is above the price of rubies; but how shall we set a value, so far as the pleasure of living is concerned, upon the power to be interesting? We hear a good deal about the highly educated young woman with reverence, about the emancipated young woman with fear and trembling, but what can take the place of the interesting woman? Anxiety is this moment agitating the minds of tens of thousands of mothers about the education of their daughters. Suppose their education should be directed to the purpose of making them interesting women, what a fascinating country this would be about the year 1900.

GIVE THE MEN A CHANCE

Give the men a chance. Upon the young women of America lies a great responsibility. The next generation will be pretty much what they choose to make it; and what are they doing for the elevation of young men? It is true that there are the colleges for men, which still perform a good work--though some of them run a good deal more to a top-dressing of accomplishments than to a sub-soiling of discipline--but these colleges reach comparatively few. There remain the great mass who are devoted to business and pleasure, and only get such intellectual cultivation as society gives them or they chance to pick up in current publications. The young women are the leisure class, consequently--so we hear--the cultivated class. Taking a certain large proportion of our society, the women in it toil not, neither do they spin; they do little or no domestic work; they engage in no productive occupation. They are set apart for a high and ennobling service--the cultivation of the mind and the rescue of society from materialism. They are the influence that keeps life elevated and sweet--are they not? For what other purpose are they set apart in elegant leisure? And nobly do they climb up to the duties of their position. They associate together in esoteric, intellectual societies. Every one is a part of many clubs, the object of which is knowledge and the broadening of the intellectual horizon. Science, languages, literature, are their daily food. They can speak in tongues; they can talk about the solar spectrum; they can interpret Chaucer, criticise Shakespeare, understand Browning. There is no literature, ancient or modern, that they do not dig up by the roots and turn over, no history that they do not drag before the club for final judgment. In every little village there is this intellectual stir and excitement; why, even in New York, readings interfere with the german;--['Dances', likely referring to the productions of the Straus family in Vienna. D.W.]--and Boston! Boston is no longer divided into wards, but into Browning "sections."

All this is mainly the work of women. The men are sometimes admitted, are even hired to perform and be encouraged and criticised; that is, men who are already highly cultivated, or who are in sympathy with the noble feminization of the age. It is a glorious movement. Its professed object is to give an intellectual lift to society. And no doubt, unless all reports are exaggerated, it is making our great leisure class of women highly intellectual beings. But, encouraging as this prospect is, it gives us pause. Who are these young women to associate with? with whom are they to hold high converse? For life is a two-fold affair. And meantime what is being done for the young men who are expected to share in the high society of the future? Will not the young women by-and-by find themselves in a lonesome place, cultivated away beyond their natural comrades? Where will they spend their evenings? This sobering thought suggests a duty that the young women are neglecting. We refer to the education of the young men. It is all very well for them to form clubs for their own advancement, and they ought not to incur the charge of selfishness in so doing; but how much better would they fulfill their mission if they would form special societies for the cultivation of young men!--sort of intellectual mission bands. Bring them into the literary circle. Make it attractive for them. Women with their attractions, not to speak of their wiles, can do anything they set out to do. They can elevate the entire present generation of young men, if they give their minds to it, to care for the intellectual pursuits they care for. Give the men a chance, and----

Musing along in this way we are suddenly pulled up by the reflection that it is impossible to make an unqualified statement that is wholly true about anything. What chance have I, anyway? inquires the young man who thinks sometimes and occasionally wants to read. What sort of leading-strings are these that I am getting into? Look at the drift of things. Is the feminization of the world a desirable thing for a vigorous future? Are the women, or are they not, taking all the virility out of literature? Answer me that. All the novels are written by, for, or about women-- brought to their standard. Even Henry James, who studies the sex untiringly, speaks about the "feminization of literature." They write most of the newspaper correspondence--and write it for women. They are even trying to feminize the colleges. Granted that woman is the superior being; all the more, what chance is there for man if this sort of thing goes on? Are you going to make a race of men on feminine fodder? And here is the still more perplexing part of it. Unless all analysis of the female heart is a delusion, and all history false, what women like most of all things in this world is a Man, virile, forceful, compelling, a solid rock of dependence, a substantial unfeminine being, whom it is some satisfaction and glory and interest to govern and rule in the right way, and twist round the feminine finger. If women should succeed in reducing or raising--of course raising--men to the feminine standard, by feminizing society, literature, the colleges, and all that, would they not turn on their creations--for even the Bible intimates that women are uncertain and go in search of a Man? It is this sort of blind instinct of the young man for preserving himself in the world that makes him so inaccessible to the good he might get from the prevailing culture of the leisure class.

THE ADVENT OF CANDOR

Those who are anxious about the fate of Christmas, whether it is not becoming too worldly and too expensive a holiday to be indulged in except by the very poor, mark with pleasure any indications that the true spirit of the day--brotherhood and self-abnegation and charity--is infusing itself into modern society. The sentimental Christmas of thirty years ago could not last; in time the manufactured jollity got to be more tedious and a greater strain on the feelings than any misfortune happening to one's neighbor. Even for a day it was very difficult to buzz about in the cheery manner prescribed, and the reaction put human nature in a bad light. Nor was it much better when gradually the day became one of Great Expectations, and the sweet spirit of it was quenched in worry or soured in disappointment. It began to take on the aspect of a great lottery, in which one class expected to draw in reverse proportion to what it put in, and another class knew that it would only reap as it had sowed. The day, blessed in its origin, and meaningless if there is a grain of selfishness in it, was thus likely to become a sort of Clearing-house of all obligations and assume a commercial aspect that took the heart out of it--like the enormous receptions for paying social debts which take the place of the old-fashioned hospitality. Everybody knew, meantime, that the spirit of good-will, the grace of universal sympathy, was really growing in the world, and that it was only our awkwardness that, by striving to cram it all for a year into twenty-four hours, made it seem a little farcical. And everybody knows that when goodness becomes fashionable, goodness is likely to suffer a little. A virtue overdone falls on t'other side. And a holiday that takes on such proportions that the Express companies and the Post-office cannot handle it is in danger of a collapse. In consideration of these things, and because, as has been pointed out year after year, Christmas is becoming a burden, the load of which is looked forward to with apprehension--and back on with nervous prostration--fear has been expressed that the dearest of all holidays in Christian lands would have to go again under a sort of Puritan protest, or into a retreat for rest and purification. We are enabled to announce for the encouragement of the single-minded in this best of all days, at the close of a year which it is best not to characterize, that those who stand upon the social watch-towers in Europe and America begin to see a light--or, it would be better to say, to perceive a spirit--in society which is likely to change many things, and; among others, to work a return of Christian simplicity. As might be expected in these days, the spirit is exhibited in the sex which is first at the wedding and last in the hospital ward. And as might have been expected, also, this spirit is shown by the young woman of the period, in whose hands are the issues of the future. If she preserve her present mind long enough, Christmas will become a day that will satisfy every human being, for the purpose of the young woman will pervade it. The tendency of the young woman generally to simplicity, of the American young woman to a certain restraint (at least when abroad), to a deference to her elders, and to tradition, has been noted. The present phenomenon is quite beyond this, and more radical. It is, one may venture to say, an attempt to conform the inner being to the outward simplicity. If one could suspect the young woman of taking up any line not original, it might be guessed that the present fashion (which is bewildering the most worldly men with a new and irresistible fascination) was set by the self-revelations of Marie Bashkirtseff. Very likely, however, it was a new spirit in the world, of which Marie was the first publishing example. Its note is self-analysis, searching, unsparing, leaving no room for the deception of self or of the world. Its leading feature is extreme candor. It is not enough to tell the truth (that has been told before); but one must act and tell the whole truth. One does not put on the shirt front and the standing collar and the knotted cravat of the other sex as a mere form; it is an act of consecration, of rigid, simple come-out-ness into the light of truth. This noble candor will suffer no concealments. She would not have her lover even, still more the general world of men, think she is better, or rather other, than she is. Not that she would like to appear a man among men, far from that; but she wishes to talk with candor and be talked to candidly, without taking advantage of that false shelter of sex behind which women have been accused of dodging. If she is nothing else, she is sincere, one might say wantonly sincere. And this lucid, candid inner life is reflected in her dress. This is not only simple in its form, in its lines; it is severe. To go into the shop of a European modiste is almost to put one's self into a truthful and candid frame of mind. Those leave frivolous ideas behind who enter here. The 'modiste' will tell the philosopher that it is now the fashion to be severe; in a word, it is 'fesch'. Nothing can go beyond that. And it symbolizes the whole life, its self-examination, earnestness, utmost candor in speech and conduct.

The statesman who is busy about his tariff and his reciprocity, and his endeavor to raise money like potatoes, may little heed and much undervalue this advent of candor into the world as a social force. But the philosopher will make no such mistake. He knows that they who build without woman build in vain, and that she is the great regenerator, as she is the great destroyer. He knows too much to disregard the gravity of any fashionable movement. He knows that there is no power on earth that can prevent the return of the long skirt. And that if the young woman has decided to be severe and candid and frank with herself and in her intercourse with others, we must submit and thank God.

And what a gift to the world is this for the Christmas season! The clear-eyed young woman of the future, always dear and often an anxiety, will this year be an object of enthusiasm.

THE AMERICAN MAN

The American man only develops himself and spreads himself and grows "for all he is worth" in the Great West. He is more free and limber there, and unfolds those generous peculiarities and largenesses of humanity which never blossomed before. The "environment" has much to do with it. The great spaces over which he roams contribute to the enlargement of his mental horizon. There have been races before who roamed the illimitable desert, but they traveled on foot or on camelback, and were limited in their range. There was nothing continental about them, as there is about our railway desert travelers, who swing along through thousands of miles of sand and sage-bush with a growing contempt for time and space. But expansive and great as these people have become under the new conditions, we have a fancy that the development of the race has only just begun, and that the future will show us in perfection a kind of man new to the world. Out somewhere on the Santa Fe route, where the desert of one day was like the desert of the day before, and the Pullman car rolls and swings over the wide waste beneath the blue sky day after day, under its black flag of smoke, in the early gray of morning, when the men were waiting their turns at the ablution bowls, a slip of a boy, perhaps aged seven, stood balancing himself on his little legs, clad in knicker-bockers, biding his time, with all the nonchalance of an old campaigner. "How did you sleep, cap?" asked a well-meaning elderly gentleman. "Well, thank you," was the dignified response; "as I always do on a sleeping-car." Always does? Great horrors! Hardly out of his swaddling-clothes, and yet he always sleeps well in a sleeper! Was he born on the wheels? was he cradled in a Pullman? He has always been in motion, probably; he was started at thirty miles an hour, no doubt, this marvelous boy of our new era. He was not born in a house at rest, but the locomotive snatched him along with a shriek and a roar before his eyes were fairly open, and he was rocked in a "section," and his first sensation of life was that of moving rapidly over vast arid spaces, through cattle ranges and along canons. The effect of quick and easy locomotion on character may have been noted before, but it seems that here is the production of a new sort of man, the direct product of our railway era. It is not simply that this boy is mature, but he must be a different and a nobler sort of boy than one born, say, at home or on a canal-boat; for, whether he was born on the rail or not, he belongs to the railway system of civilization. Before he gets into trousers he is old in experience, and he has discounted many of the novelties that usually break gradually on the pilgrim in this world. He belongs to the new expansive race that must live in motion, whose proper home is the Pullman (which will probably be improved in time into a dustless, sweet-smelling, well-aired bed-room), and whose domestic life will be on the wing, so to speak. The Inter-State Commerce Bill will pass him along without friction from end to end of the Union, and perhaps a uniform divorce law will enable him to change his marital relations at any place where he happens to dine. This promising lad is only a faint intimation of what we are all coming to when we fully acquire the freedom of the continent, and come into that expansiveness of feeling and of language which characterizes the Great West. It is a burst of joyous exuberance that comes from the sense of an il-limitable horizon. It shows itself in the tender words of a local newspaper at Bowie, Arizona, on the death of a beloved citizen: "'Death loves a shining mark,' and she hit a dandy when she turned loose on Jim." And also in the closing words of a New Mexico obituary, which the Kansas Magazine quotes: "Her tired spirit was released from the pain-racking body and soared aloft to eternal glory at 4.30 Denver time." We die, as it were, in motion, as we sleep, and there is nowhere any boundary to our expansion. Perhaps we shall never again know any rest as we now understand the term--rest being only change of motion--and we shall not be able to sleep except on the cars, and whether we die by Denver time or by the 90th meridian, we shall only change our time. Blessed be this slip of a boy who is a man before he is an infant, and teaches us what rapid transit can do for our race! The only thing that can possibly hinder us in our progress will be second childhood; we have abolished first.

THE ELECTRIC WAY

We are quite in the electric way. We boast that we have made electricity our slave, but the slave whom we do not understand is our master. And before we know him we shall be transformed. Mr. Edison proposes to send us over the country at the rate of one hundred miles an hour. This pleases us, because we fancy we shall save time, and because we are taught that the chief object in life is to "get there" quickly. We really have an idea that it is a gain to annihilate distance, forgetting that as a matter of personal experience we are already too near most people. But this speed by rail will enable us to live in Philadelphia and do business in New York. It will make the city of Chicago two hundred miles square. And the bigger Chicago is, the more important this world becomes. This pleasing anticipation--that of traveling by lightning, and all being huddled together--is nothing to the promised universal illumination by a diffused light that shall make midnight as bright as noonday. We shall then save all the time there is, and at the age of thirty-five have lived the allotted seventy years, and long, if not for 'Gotterdammerung', at least for some world where, by touching a button, we can discharge our limbs of electricity and take a little repose. The most restless and ambitious of us can hardly conceive of Chicago as a desirable future state of existence.

This, however, is only the external or superficial view of the subject; at the best it is only symbolical. Mr. Edison is wasting his time in objective experiments, while we are in the deepest ignorance as to our electric personality or our personal electricity. We begin to apprehend that we are electric beings, that these outward manifestations of a subtile form are only hints of our internal state. Mr. Edison should turn his attention from physics to humanity electrically considered in its social condition. We have heard a great deal about affinities. We are told that one person is positive and another negative, and that representing socially opposite poles they should come together and make an electric harmony, that two positives or two negatives repel each other, and if conventionally united end in divorce, and so on. We read that such a man is magnetic, meaning that he can poll a great many votes; or that such a woman thrilled her audience, meaning probably that they were in an electric condition to be shocked by her. Now this is what we want to find out--to know if persons are really magnetic or sympathetic, and how to tell whether a person is positive or negative. In politics we are quite at sea. What is the good of sending a man to Washington at the rate of a hundred miles an hour if we are uncertain of his electric state? The ideal House of Representatives ought to be pretty nearly balanced--half positive, half negative. Some Congresses seem to be made up pretty much of negatives. The time for the electrician to test the candidate is before he is put in nomination, not dump him into Congress as we do now, utterly ignorant of whether his currents run from his heels to his head or from his head to his heels, uncertain, indeed, as to whether he has magnetism to run in at all. Nothing could be more unscientific than the process and the result.

In social life it is infinitely worse. You, an electric unmarried man, enter a room full of attractive women. How are you to know who is positive and who is negative, or who is a maiden lady in equilibrium, if it be true, as scientists affirm, that the genus old maid is one in whom the positive currents neutralize the negative currents? Your affinity is perhaps the plainest woman in the room. But beauty is a juggling sprite, entirely uncontrolled by electricity, and you are quite likely to make a mistake. It is absurd the way we blunder on in a scientific age. We touch a button, and are married. The judge touches another button, and we are divorced. If when we touched the first button it revealed us both negatives, we should start back in horror, for it is only before engagement that two negatives make an affirmative. That is the reason that some clergymen refuse to marry a divorced woman; they see that she has made one electric mistake, and fear she will make another. It is all very well for the officiating clergyman to ask the two intending to commit matrimony if they have a license from the town clerk, if they are of age or have the consent of parents, and have a million; but the vital point is omitted. Are they electric affinities? It should be the duty of the town-clerk, by a battery, or by some means to be discovered by electricians, to find out the galvanic habit of the parties, their prevailing electric condition. Temporarily they may seem to be in harmony, and may deceive themselves into the belief that they are at opposite poles equidistant from the equator, and certain to meet on that imaginary line in matrimonial bliss. Dreadful will be the awakening to an insipid life, if they find they both have the same sort of currents. It is said that women change their minds and their dispositions, that men are fickle, and that both give way after marriage to natural inclinations that were suppressed while they were on the good behavior that the supposed necessity of getting married imposes. This is so notoriously true that it ought to create a public panic. But there is hope in the new light. If we understand it, persons are born in a certain electrical condition, and substantially continue in it, however much they may apparently wobble about under the influence of infirm minds and acquired wickedness. There are, of course, variations of the compass to be reckoned with, and the magnet may occasionally be bewitched by near and powerful attracting objects. But, on the whole, the magnet remains the same, and it is probable that a person's normal electric condition is the thing in him least liable to dangerous variation. If this be true, the best basis for matrimony is the electric, and our social life would have fewer disappointments if men and women went about labeled with their scientifically ascertained electric qualities.

CAN A HUSBAND OPEN HIS WIFE'S LETTERS?

Can a husband open his wife's letters? That would depend, many would say, upon what kind of a husband he is. But it cannot be put aside in that flippant manner, for it is a legal right that is in question, and it has recently been decided in a Paris tribunal that the husband has the right to open the letters addressed to his wife. Of course in America an appeal would instantly be taken from this decision, and perhaps by husbands themselves; for in this world rights are becoming so impartially distributed that this privilege granted to the husband might at once be extended to the wife, and she would read all his business correspondence, and his business is sometimes various and complicated. The Paris decision must be based upon the familiar formula that man and wife are one, and that that one is the husband. If a man has the right to read all the letters written to his wife, being his property by reason of his ownership of her, why may he not have a legal right to know all that is said to her? The question is not whether a wife ought to receive letters that her husband may not read, or listen to talk that he may not hear, but whether he has a sort of lordship that gives him privileges which she does not enjoy. In our modern notion of marriage, which is getting itself expressed in statute law, marriage is supposed to rest on mutual trust and mutual rights. In theory the husband and wife are still one, and there can nothing come into the life of one that is not shared by the other; in fact, if the marriage is perfect and the trust absolute, the personality of each is respected by the other, and each is freely the judge of what shall be contributed to the common confidence; and if there are any concealments, it is well believed that they are for the mutual good. If every one were as perfect in the marriage relation as those who are reading these lines, the question of the wife's letters would never arise. The man, trusting his wife, would not care to pry into any little secrets his wife might have, or bother himself about her correspondence; he would know, indeed, that if he had lost her real affection, a surveillance of her letters could not restore it.

Perhaps it is a modern notion that marriage is a union of trust and not of suspicion, of expectation of faithfulness the more there is freedom. At any rate, the tendency, notwithstanding the French decision, is away from the common-law suspicion and tyranny towards a higher trust in an enlarged freedom. And it is certain that the rights cannot all be on one side and the duties on the other. If the husband legally may compel his wife to show him her letters, the courts will before long grant the same privilege to the wife. But, without pressing this point, we hold strongly to the sacredness of correspondence. The letters one receives are in one sense not his own. They contain the confessions of another soul, the confidences of another mind, that would be rudely treated if given any sort of publicity. And while husband and wife are one to each other, they are two in the eyes of other people, and it may well happen that a friend will desire to impart something to a discreet woman which she would not intrust to the babbling husband of that woman. Every life must have its own privacy and its own place of retirement. The letter is of all things the most personal and intimate thing. Its bloom is gone when another eye sees it before the one for which it was intended. Its aroma all escapes when it is first opened by another person. One might as well wear second-hand clothing as get a second-hand letter. Here, then, is a sacred right that ought to be respected, and can be respected without any injury to domestic life. The habit in some families for the members of it to show each other's letters is a most disenchanting one. It is just in the family, between persons most intimate, that these delicacies of consideration for the privacy of each ought to be most respected. No one can estimate probably how much of the refinement, of the delicacy of feeling, has been lost to the world by the introduction of the postal-card. Anything written on a postal-card has no personality; it is banal, and has as little power of charming any one who receives it as an advertisement in the newspaper. It is not simply the cheapness of the communication that is vulgar, but the publicity of it. One may have perhaps only a cent's worth of affection to send, but it seems worth much more when enclosed in an envelope. We have no doubt, then, that on general principles the French decision is a mistake, and that it tends rather to vulgarize than to retain the purity and delicacy of the marriage relation. And the judges, so long even as men only occupy the bench, will no doubt reverse it when the logical march of events forces upon them the question whether the wife may open her husband's letters.

A LEISURE CLASS

Foreign critics have apologized for real or imagined social and literary short-comings in this country on the ground that the American people have little leisure. It is supposed that when we have a leisure class we shall not only make a better showing in these respects, but we shall be as agreeable--having time to devote to the art of being agreeable--as the English are. But we already have a considerable and increasing number of people who can command their own time if we have not a leisure class, and the sociologist might begin to study the effect of this leisureliness upon society. Are the people who, by reason of a competence or other accidents of good-fortune, have most leisure, becoming more agreeable? and are they devoting themselves to the elevation of the social tone, or to the improvement of our literature? However this question is answered, a strong appeal might be made to the people of leisure to do not only what is expected of them by foreign observers, but to take advantage of their immense opportunities. In a republic there is no room for a leisure class that is not useful. Those who use their time merely to kill it, in imitation of those born to idleness and to no necessity of making an exertion, may be ornamental, but having no root in any established privilege to sustain them, they will soon wither away in this atmosphere, as a flower would which should set up to be an orchid when it does not belong to the orchid family. It is required here that those who are emancipated from the daily grind should vindicate their right to their position not only by setting an example of self-culture, but by contributing something to the general welfare. It is thought by many that if society here were established and settled as it is elsewhere, the rich would be less dominated by their money and less conscious of it, and having leisure, could devote themselves even more than they do now to intellectual and spiritual pursuits.

Whether these anticipations will ever be realized, and whether increased leisure will make us all happy, is a subject of importance; but it is secondary, and in a manner incidental, to another and deeper matter, which may be defined as the responsibility of attractiveness. And this responsibility takes two forms the duty of every one to be attractive, and the danger of being too attractive. To be winning and agreeable is sometimes reckoned a gift, but it is a disposition that can be cultivated; and, in a world so given to grippe and misapprehension as this is, personal attractiveness becomes a duty, if it is not an art, that might be taught in the public schools. It used to be charged against New Englanders that they regarded this gift as of little value, and were inclined to hide it under a bushel, and it was said of some of their neighbors in the Union that they exaggerated its importance, and neglected the weightier things of the law. Indeed, disputes have arisen as to what attractiveness consisted in--some holding that beauty or charm of manner (which is almost as good) and sweetness and gayety were sufficient, while others held that a little intelligence sprinkled in was essential. But one thing is clear, that while women were held to strict responsibility in this matter, not stress enough was laid upon the equal duty of men to be attractive in order to make the world agreeable. Hence it is, probably, that while no question has been raised as to the effect of the higher education upon the attractiveness of men, the colleges for girls have been jealously watched as to the effect they were likely to have upon the attractiveness of women. Whether the college years of a young man, during which he knows more than he will ever know again, are his most attractive period is not considered, for he is expected to develop what is in him later on; but it is gravely questioned whether girls who give their minds to the highest studies are not dropping those graces of personal attractiveness which they will find it difficult to pick up again. Of course such a question as this could never arise except in just such a world as this is. For in an ideal world it could be shown that the highest intelligence and the highest personal charm are twins. If, therefore, it should turn out, which seems absurd, that college-educated girls are not as attractive as other women with less advantages, it will have to be admitted that something is the matter with the young ladies, which is preposterous, or that the system is still defective. For the postulate that everybody ought to be attractive cannot be abandoned for the sake of any system. Decision on this system cannot be reached without long experience, for it is always to be remembered that the man's point of view of attractiveness may shift, and he may come to regard the intellectual graces as supremely attractive; while, on the other hand, the woman student may find that a winning smile is just as effective in bringing a man to her feet, where he belongs, as a logarithm.

The danger of being too attractive, though it has historic illustration, is thought by many to be more apparent than real. Merely being too attractive has often been confounded with a love of flirtation and conquest, unbecoming always in a man, and excused in a woman on the ground of her helplessness. It could easily be shown that to use personal attractiveness recklessly to the extent of hopeless beguilement is cruel, and it may be admitted that woman ought to be held to strict responsibility for her attractiveness. The lines are indeed hard for her. The duty is upon her in this poor world of being as attractive as she can, and yet she is held responsible for all the mischief her attractiveness produces. As if the blazing sun should be called to account by people with weak eyes.

WEATHER AND CHARACTER

The month of February in all latitudes in the United States is uncertain. The birth of George Washington in it has not raised it in public esteem. In the North, it is a month to flee from; in the South, at best it is a waiting month--a month of rain and fickle skies. A good deal has been done for it. It is the month of St. Valentine, it is distinguished by the leap-year addition of a day, and ought to be a favorite of the gentle sex; but it remains a sort of off period in the year. Its brevity recommends it, but no one would take any notice of it were it not for its effect upon character. A month of rigid weather is supposed to brace up the moral nature, and a month of gentleness is supposed to soften the asperities of the disposition, but February contributes to neither of these ends. It is neither a tonic nor a soother; that is, in most parts of our inexplicable land. We make no complaint of this. It is probably well to have a period in the year that tests character to the utmost, and the person who can enter spring through the gate of February a better man or woman is likely to adorn society the rest of the year. February, however, is merely an illustration of the effect of weather upon the disposition. Persons differ in regard to their sensitiveness to cloudy, rainy, and gloomy days. We recognize this in a general way, but the relation of temper and disposition to the weather has never been scientifically studied. Our observation of the influence of climate is mostly with regard to physical infirmities. We know the effect of damp weather upon rheumatics, and of the east wind upon gouty subjects, but too little allowance is made for the influence of weather upon the spirits and the conduct of men. We know that a long period of gloomy weather leads to suicides, and we observe that long-continued clouds and rain beget "crossness" and ill-temper, and we are all familiar with the universal exhilaration of sunshine and clear air upon any company of men and women. But the point we wish to make is that neither society nor the law makes any allowance for the aberrations of human nature caused by dull and unpleasant weather. And this is very singular in this humanitarian age, when excuse is found for nearly every moral delinquency in heredity or environment, that the greatest factor of discontent and crookedness, the weather, should be left out of consideration altogether. The relation of crime to the temperature and the humidity of the atmosphere is not taken into account. Yet crime and eccentricity of conduct are very much the result of atmospheric conditions, since they depend upon the temper and the spirit of the community. Many people are habitually blue and down-hearted in sour weather; a long spell of cloudy, damp, cold weather depresses everybody, lowers hope, tends to melancholy; and people when they are not cheerful are more apt to fall into evil ways, as a rule, than when they are in a normal state of good-humor. And aside from crimes, the vexation, the friction, the domestic discontent in life, are provoked by bad weather. We should like to have some statistics as to incompatibility between married couples produced by damp and raw days, and to know whether divorces are more numerous in the States that suffer from a fickle climate than in those where the climate is more equable. It is true that in the Sandwich Islands and in Egypt there is greater mental serenity, less perturbation of spirit, less worry, than in the changeable United States. Something of this placidity and resignation to the ills inevitable in human life is due to an even climate, to the constant sun and the dry air. We cannot hope to prevent crime and suffering by statistics, any more than we have been able to improve our climate (which is rather worse now than before the scientists took it in charge) by observations and telegraphic reports; but we can, by careful tabulation of the effects of bad weather upon the spirits of a community, learn what places in the Union are favorable to the production of cheerfulness and an equal mind. And we should lift a load of reprobation from some places which now have a reputation for surliness and unamiability. We find the people of one place hospitable, lighthearted, and agreeable; the people of another place cold, and morose, and unpleasant. It would be a satisfaction to know that the weather is responsible for the difference. Observation of this sort would also teach us doubtless what places are most conducive to literary production, what to happy homes and agreeing wives and husbands. All our territory is mapped out as to its sanitary conditions; why not have it colored as to its effect upon the spirits and the enjoyment of life? The suggestion opens a vast field of investigation.

BORN WITH AN "EGO"

There used to be a notion going round that it would be a good thing for people if they were more "self-centred." Perhaps there was talk of adding a course to the college curriculum, in addition to that for training the all-competent "journalist," for the self-centring of the young. To apply the term to a man or woman was considered highly complimentary. The advisers of this state of mind probably meant to suggest a desirable equilibrium and mental balance; but the actual effect of the self-centred training is illustrated by a story told of Thomas H. Benton, who had been described as an egotist by some of the newspapers. Meeting Colonel Frank Blair one day, he said: "Colonel Blair, I see that the newspapers call me an egotist. I wish you would tell me frankly, as a friend, if you think the charge is true." "It is a very direct question, Mr. Benton," replied Colonel Blair, "but if you want my honest opinion, I am compelled to say that I think there is some foundation for the charge." "Well, sir," said Mr. Benton, throwing his head back and his chest forward, "the difference between me and these little fellows is that I have an EGO!" Mr. Benton was an interesting man, and it is a fair consideration if a certain amount of egotism does not add to the interest of any character, but at the same time the self-centred conditions shut a person off from one of the chief enjoyments to be got out of this world, namely, a recognition of what is admirable in others in a toleration of peculiarities. It is odd, almost amusing, to note how in this country people of one section apply their local standards to the judgment of people in other sections, very much as an Englishman uses his insular yardstick to measure all the rest of the world. It never seems to occur to people in one locality that the manners and speech of those of another may be just as admirable as their own, and they get a good deal of discomfort out of their intercourse with strangers by reason of their inability to adapt themselves to any ways not their own. It helps greatly to make this country interesting that nearly every State has its peculiarities, and that the inhabitants of different sections differ in manner and speech. But next to an interesting person in social value, is an agreeable one, and it would add vastly to the agreeableness of life if our widely spread provinces were not so self-centred in their notion that their own way is the best, to the degree that they criticise any deviation from it as an eccentricity. It would be a very nice world in these United States if we could all devote ourselves to finding out in communities what is likable rather than what is opposed to our experience; that is, in trying to adapt ourselves to others rather than insisting that our own standard should measure our opinion and our enjoyment of them.

When the Kentuckian describes a man as a "high-toned gentleman" he means exactly the same that a Bostonian means when, he says that a man is a "very good fellow," only the men described have a different culture, a different personal flavor; and it is fortunate that the Kentuckian is not like the Bostonian, for each has a quality that makes intercourse with him pleasant. In the South many people think they have said a severe thing when they say that a person or manner is thoroughly Yankee; and many New Englanders intend to express a considerable lack in what is essential when they say of men and women that they are very Southern. When the Yankee is produced he may turn out a cosmopolitan person of the most interesting and agreeable sort; and the Southerner may have traits and peculiarities, growing out of climate and social life unlike the New England, which are altogether charming. We talked once with a Western man of considerable age and experience who had the placid mind that is sometimes, and may more and more become, the characteristic of those who live in flat countries of illimitable horizons, who said that New Yorkers, State and city, all had an assertive sort of smartness that was very disagreeable to him. And a lady of New York (a city whose dialect the novelists are beginning to satirize) was much disturbed by the flatness of speech prevailing in Chicago, and thought something should be done in the public schools to correct the pronunciation of English. There doubtless should be a common standard of distinct, rounded, melodious pronunciation, as there is of good breeding, and it is quite as important to cultivate the voice in speaking as in singing, but the people of the United States let themselves be immensely irritated by local differences and want of toleration of sectional peculiarities. The truth is that the agreeable people are pretty evenly distributed over the country, and one's enjoyment of them is heightened not only by their differences of manner, but by the different, ways in which they look at life, unless he insists upon applying everywhere the yardstick of his own locality. If the Boston woman sets her eyeglasses at a critical angle towards the 'laisser faire' flow of social amenity in New Orleans, and the New Orleans woman seeks out only the prim and conventional in Boston, each may miss the opportunity to supplement her life by something wanting and desirable in it, to be gained by the exercise of more openness of mind and toleration. To some people Yankee thrift is disagreeable; to others, Southern shiftlessness is intolerable. To some travelers the negro of the South, with his tropical nature, his capacity for picturesque attitudes, his abundant trust in Providence, is an element of restfulness; and if the chief object of life is happiness, the traveler may take a useful hint from the race whose utmost desire, in a fit climate, would be fully satisfied by a shirt and a banana-tree. But to another traveler the dusky, careless race is a continual affront.

If a person is born with an "Ego," and gets the most enjoyment out of the world by trying to make it revolve about himself, and cannot make-allowances for differences, we have nothing to say except to express pity for such a self-centred condition; which shuts him out of the never-failing pleasure there is in entering into and understanding with sympathy the almost infinite variety in American life.

JUVENTUS MUNDI

Sometimes the world seems very old. It appeared so to Bernard of Cluny in the twelfth century, when he wrote:

"The world is very evil,
The times are waning late."

There was a general impression among the Christians of the first century of our era that the end was near. The world must have seemed very ancient to the Egyptians fifteen hundred years before Christ, when the Pyramid of Cheops was a relic of antiquity, when almost the whole circle of arts, sciences, and literature had been run through, when every nation within reach had been conquered, when woman had been developed into one of the most fascinating of beings, and even reigned more absolutely than Elizabeth or Victoria has reigned since: it was a pretty tired old world at that time. One might almost say that the further we go back the older and more "played out" the world appears, notwithstanding that the poets, who were generally pessimists of the present, kept harping about the youth of the world and the joyous spontaneity of human life in some golden age before their time. In fact, the world is old in spots--in Memphis and Boston and Damascus and Salem and Ephesus. Some of these places are venerable in traditions, and some of them are actually worn out and taking a rest from too much civilization--lying fallow, as the saying is. But age is so entirely relative that to many persons the landing of the Mayflower seems more remote than the voyage of Jason, and a Mayflower chest a more antique piece of furniture than the timbers of the Ark, which some believe can still be seen on top of Mount Ararat. But, speaking generally, the world is still young and growing, and a considerable portion of it unfinished. The oldest part, indeed, the Laurentian Hills, which were first out of water, is still only sparsely settled; and no one pretends that Florida is anything like finished, or that the delta of the Mississippi is in anything more than the process of formation. Men are so young and lively in these days that they cannot wait for the slow processes of nature, but they fill up and bank up places, like Holland, where they can live; and they keep on exploring and discovering incongruous regions, like Alaska, where they can go and exercise their juvenile exuberance.

In many respects the world has been growing younger ever since the Christian era. A new spirit came into it then which makes youth perpetual, a spirit of living in others, which got the name of universal brotherhood, a spirit that has had a good many discouragements and set-backs, but which, on the whole, gains ground, and generally works in harmony with the scientific spirit, breaking down the exclusive character of the conquests of nature. What used to be the mystery and occultism of the few is now general knowledge, so that all the playing at occultism by conceited people now seems jejune and foolish. A little machine called the instantaneous photograph takes pictures as quickly and accurately as the human eye does, and besides makes them permanent. Instead of fooling credulous multitudes with responses from Delphi, we have a Congress which can enact tariff regulations susceptible of interpretations enough to satisfy the love of mystery of the entire nation. Instead of loafing round Memnon at sunrise to catch some supernatural tones, we talk words into a little contrivance which will repeat our words and tones to the remotest generation of those who shall be curious to know whether we said those words in jest or earnest. All these mysteries made common and diffused certainly increase the feeling of the equality of opportunity in the world. And day by day such wonderful things are discovered and scattered abroad that we are warranted in believing that we are only on the threshold of turning to account the hidden forces of nature. There would be great danger of human presumption and conceit in this progress if the conceit were not so widely diffused, and where we are all conceited there is no one to whom it will appear unpleasant. If there was only one person who knew about the telephone he would be unbearable. Probably the Eiffel Tower would be stricken down as a monumental presumption, like that of Babel, if it had not been raised with the full knowledge and consent of all the world.

This new spirit, with its multiform manifestations, which came into the world nearly nineteen hundred years ago, is sometimes called the spirit of Christmas. And good reasons can be given for supposing that it is. At any rate, those nations that have the most of it are the most prosperous, and those people who have the most of it are the most agreeable to associate with. Know all men by these Presents, is an old legal form which has come to have a new meaning in this dispensation. It is by the spirit of brotherhood exhibited in giving presents that we know the Christmas proper, only we are apt to take it in too narrow a way. The real spirit of Christmas is the general diffusion of helpfulness and good-will. If somebody were to discover an elixir which would make every one truthful, he would not, in this age of the world, patent it. Indeed, the Patent Office would not let him make a corner on virtue as he does in wheat; and it is not respectable any more among the real children of Christmas to make a corner in wheat. The world, to be sure, tolerates still a great many things that it does not approve of, and, on the whole, Christmas, as an ameliorating and good-fellowship institution, gains a little year by year. There is still one hitch about it, and a bad one just now, namely, that many people think they can buy its spirit by jerks of liberality, by costly gifts. Whereas the fact is that a great many of the costliest gifts in this season do not count at all. Crumbs from the rich man's table don't avail any more to open the pearly gates even of popular esteem in this world. Let us say, in fine, that a loving, sympathetic heart is better than a nickel-plated service in this world, which is surely growing young and sympathetic.

A BEAUTIFUL OLD AGE

In Autumn the thoughts lightly turn to Age. If the writer has seemed to be interested, sometimes to the neglect of other topics, in the American young woman, it was not because she is interested in herself, but because she is on the way to be one of the most agreeable objects in this lovely world. She may struggle against it; she may resist it by all the legitimate arts of the coquette and the chemist; she may be convinced that youth and beauty are inseparable allies; but she would have more patience if she reflected that the sunset is often finer than the sunrise, commonly finer than noon, especially after a stormy day. The secret of a beautiful old age is as well worth seeking as that of a charming young maidenhood. For it is one of the compensations for the rest of us, in the decay of this mortal life, that women, whose mission it is to allure in youth and to tinge the beginning of the world with romance, also make the end of the world more serenely satisfactory and beautiful than the outset. And this has been done without any amendment to the Constitution of the United States; in fact, it is possible that the Sixteenth Amendment would rather hinder than help this gracious process. We are not speaking now of what is called growing old gracefully and regretfully, as something to be endured, but as a season to be desired for itself, at least by those whose privilege it is to be ennobled and cheered by it. And we are not speaking of wicked old women. There is a unique fascination--all the novelists recognize it--in a wicked old woman; not very wicked, but a woman of abundant experience, who is perfectly frank and a little cynical, and delights in probing human nature and flashing her wit on its weaknesses, and who knows as much about life as a club man is credited with knowing. She may not be a good comrade for the young, but she is immensely more fascinating than a semi-wicked old man. Why, we do not know; that is one of the unfathomable mysteries of womanhood. No; we have in mind quite another sort of woman, of which America has so many that they are a very noticeable element in all cultivated society. And the world has nothing more lovely. For there is a loveliness or fascination sometimes in women between the ages of sixty and eighty that is unlike any other--a charm that woos us to regard autumn as beautiful as spring.

Perhaps these women were great beauties in their day, but scarcely so serenely beautiful as now when age has refined all that was most attractive. Perhaps they were plain; but it does not matter, for the subtle influence of spiritualized-intelligence has the power of transforming plainness into the beauty of old age. Physical beauty is doubtless a great advantage, and it is never lost if mind shines through it (there is nothing so unlovely as a frivolous old woman fighting to keep the skin-deep beauty of her youth); the eyes, if the life has not been one of physical suffering, usually retain their power of moving appeal; the lines of the face, if changed, may be refined by a certain spirituality; the gray hair gives dignity and softness and the charm of contrast; the low sweet voice vibrates to the same note of femininity, and the graceful and gracious are graceful and gracious still. Even into the face and bearing of the plain woman whose mind has grown, whose thoughts have been pure, whose heart has been expanded by good deeds or by constant affection, comes a beauty winning and satisfactory in the highest degree.

It is not that the charm of the women of whom we speak is mainly this physical beauty; that is only incidental, as it were. The delight in their society has a variety of sources. Their interest in life is broader than it once was, more sympathetically unselfish; they have a certain philosophical serenity that is not inconsistent with great liveliness of mind; they have got rid of so much nonsense; they can afford to be truthful--and how much there is to be learned from a woman who is truthful! they have a most delicious courage of opinion, about men, say, and in politics, and social topics, and creeds even. They have very little any longer to conceal; that is, in regard to things that should be thought about and talked about at all. They are not afraid to be gay, and to have enthusiasms. At sixty and eighty a refined and well-bred woman is emancipated in the best way, and in the enjoyment of the full play of the richest qualities of her womanhood. She is as far from prudery as from the least note of vulgarity. Passion, perhaps, is replaced by a great capacity for friendliness, and she was never more a real woman than in these mellow and reflective days. And how interesting she is--adding so much knowledge of life to the complex interest that inheres in her sex! Knowledge of life, yes, and of affairs; for it must be said of these ladies we have in mind that they keep up with the current thought, that they are readers of books, even of newspapers--for even the newspaper can be helpful and not harmful in the alembic of their minds.

Let not the purpose of this paper be misunderstood. It is not to urge young women to become old or to act like old women. The independence and frankness of age might not be becoming to them. They must stumble along as best they can, alternately attracting and repelling, until by right of years they join that serene company which is altogether beautiful. There is a natural unfolding and maturing to the beauty of old age. The mission of woman, about which we are pretty weary of hearing, is not accomplished by any means in her years of vernal bloom and loveliness; she has equal power to bless and sweeten life in the autumn of her pilgrimage. But here is an apologue: The peach, from blossom to maturity, is the most attractive of fruits. Yet the demands of the market, competition, and fashion often cause it to be plucked and shipped while green. It never matures, though it may take a deceptive richness of color; it decays without ripening. And the last end of that peach is worse than the first.

THE ATTRACTION OF THE REPULSIVE

On one of the most charming of the many wonderfully picturesque little beaches on the Pacific coast, near Monterey, is the idlest if not the most disagreeable social group in the world. Just off the shore, farther than a stone's-throw, lies a mass of broken rocks. The surf comes leaping and laughing in, sending up, above the curving green breakers and crests of foam, jets and spirals of water which flash like silver fountains in the sunlight. These islets of rocks are the homes of the sea-lion. This loafer of the coast congregates here by the thousand. Sometimes the rocks are quite covered, the smooth rounded surface of the larger one presenting the appearance at a distance of a knoll dotted with dirty sheep. There is generally a select knot of a dozen floating about in the still water under the lee of the rock, bobbing up their tails and flippers very much as black driftwood might heave about in the tide. During certain parts of the day members of this community are off fishing in deep water; but what they like best to do is to crawl up on the rocks and grunt and bellow, or go to sleep in the sun. Some of them lie half in water, their tails floating and their ungainly heads wagging. These uneasy ones are always wriggling out or plunging in. Some crawl to the tops of the rocks and lie like gunny bags stuffed with meal, or they repose on the broken surfaces like masses of jelly. When they are all at home the rocks have not room for them, and they crawl on and over each other, and lie like piles of undressed pork. In the water they are black, but when they are dry in the sun the skin becomes a dirty light brown. Many of them are huge fellows, with a body as big as an ox. In the water they are repulsively graceful; on the rocks they are as ungainly as boneless cows, or hogs that have lost their shape in prosperity. Summer and winter (and it is almost always summer on this coast) these beasts, which are well fitted neither for land nor water, spend their time in absolute indolence, except when they are compelled to cruise around in the deep water for food. They are of no use to anybody, either for their skin or their flesh. Nothing could be more thoroughly disgusting and uncanny than they are, and yet nothing more fascinating. One can watch them--the irresponsible, formless lumps of intelligent flesh--for hours without tiring. I scarcely know what the fascination is. A small seal playing by himself near the shore, floating on and diving under the breakers, is not so very disagreeable, especially if he comes so near that you can see his pathetic eyes; but these brutes in this perpetual summer resort are disgustingly attractive. Nearly everything about them, including their voice, is repulsive. Perhaps it is the absolute idleness of the community that makes it so interesting. To fish, to swim, to snooze on the rocks, that is all, for ever and ever. No past, no future. A society that lives for the laziest sort of pleasure. If they were rich, what more could they have? Is not this the ideal of a watering-place life?

The spectacle of this happy community ought to teach us humility and charity in judgment. Perhaps the philosophy of its attractiveness lies deeper than its 'dolce far niente' existence. We may never have considered the attraction for us of the disagreeable, the positive fascination of the uncommonly ugly. The repulsive fascination of the loathly serpent or dragon for women can hardly be explained on theological grounds. Some cranks have maintained that the theory of gravitation alone does not explain the universe, that repulsion is as necessary as attraction in our economy. This may apply to society. We are all charmed with the luxuriance of a semi-tropical landscape, so violently charmed that we become in time tired of its overpowering bloom and color. But what is the charm of the wide, treeless desert, the leagues of sand and burnt-up chaparral, the distant savage, fantastic mountains, the dry desolation as of a world burnt out? It is not contrast altogether. For this illimitable waste has its own charm; and again and again, when we come to a world of vegetation, where the vision is shut in by beauty, we shall have an irrepressible longing for these wind-swept plains as wide as the sea, with the ashy and pink horizons. We shall long to be weary of it all again--its vast nakedness, its shimmering heat, its cold, star-studded nights. It seems paradoxical, but it is probably true, that a society composed altogether of agreeable people would become a terrible bore. We are a "kittle" lot, and hard to please for long. We know how it is in the matter of climate. Why is it that the masses of the human race live in the most disagreeable climates to be found on the globe, subject to extremes of heat and cold, sudden and unprovoked changes, frosts, fogs, malarias? In such regions they congregate, and seem to like the vicissitudes, to like the excitement of the struggle with the weather and the patent medicines to keep alive. They hate the agreeable monotony of one genial day following another the year through. They praise this monotony, all literature is full of it; people always say they are in search of the equable climate; but they continue to live, nevertheless, or try to live, in the least equable; and if they can find one spot more disagreeable than another there they build a big city. If man could make his ideal climate he would probably be dissatisfied with it in a month. The effect of climate upon disposition and upon manners needs to be considered some day; but we are now only trying to understand the attractiveness of the disagreeable. There must be some reason for it; and that would explain a social phenomenon, why there are so many unattractive people, and why the attractive readers of these essays could not get on without them.

The writer of this once traveled for days with an intelligent curmudgeon, who made himself at all points as prickly as the porcupine. There was no getting on with him. And yet when he dropped out of the party he was sorely missed. He was more attractively repulsive than the sea-lion. It was such a luxury to hate him. He was such a counter-irritant, such a stimulant; such a flavor he gave to life. We are always on the lookout for the odd, the eccentric, the whimsical. We pretend that we like the orderly, the beautiful, the pleasant. We can find them anywhere--the little bits of scenery that please the eye, the pleasant households, the group of delightful people. Why travel, then? We want the abnormal, the strong, the ugly, the unusual at least. We wish to be startled and stirred up and repelled. And we ought to be more thankful than we are that there are so many desolate and wearisome and fantastic places, and so many tiresome and unattractive people in this lovely world.

GIVING AS A LUXURY

There must be something very good in human nature, or people would not experience so much pleasure in giving; there must be something very bad in human nature, or more people would try the experiment of giving. Those who do try it become enamored of it, and get their chief pleasure in life out of it; and so evident is this that there is some basis for the idea that it is ignorance rather than badness which keeps so many people from being generous. Of course it may become a sort of dissipation, or more than that, a devastation, as many men who have what are called "good wives" have reason to know, in the gradual disappearance of their wardrobe if they chance to lay aside any of it temporarily. The amount that a good woman can give away is only measured by her opportunity. Her mind becomes so trained in the mystery of this pleasure that she experiences no thrill of delight in giving away only the things her husband does not want. Her office in life is to teach him the joy of self-sacrifice. She and all other habitual and irreclaimable givers soon find out that there is next to no pleasure in a gift unless it involves some self-denial.

Let one consider seriously whether he ever gets as much satisfaction out of a gift received as out of one given. It pleases him for the moment, and if it is useful, for a long time; he turns it over, and admires it; he may value it as a token of affection, and it flatters his self-esteem that he is the object of it. But it is a transient feeling compared with that he has when he has made a gift. That substantially ministers to his self-esteem. He follows the gift; he dwells upon the delight of the receiver; his imagination plays about it; it will never wear out or become stale; having parted with it, it is for him a lasting possession. It is an investment as lasting as that in the debt of England. Like a good deed, it grows, and is continually satisfactory. It is something to think of when he first wakes in the morning--a time when most people are badly put to it for want of something pleasant to think of. This fact about giving is so incontestably true that it is a wonder that enlightened people do not more freely indulge in giving for their own comfort. It is, above all else, amazing that so many imagine they are going to get any satisfaction out of what they leave by will. They may be in a state where they will enjoy it, if the will is not fought over; but it is shocking how little gratitude there is accorded to a departed giver compared to a living giver. He couldn't take the property with him, it is said; he was obliged to leave it to somebody. By this thought his generosity is always reduced to a minimum. He may build a monument to himself in some institution, but we do not know enough of the world to which he has gone to know whether a tiny monument on this earth is any satisfaction to a person who is free of the universe. Whereas every giving or deed of real humanity done while he was living would have entered into his character, and would be of lasting service to him--that is, in any future which we can conceive.

Of course we are not confining our remarks to what are called Christmas gifts--commercially so called--nor would we undertake to estimate the pleasure there is in either receiving or giving these. The shrewd manufacturers of the world have taken notice of the periodic generosity of the race, and ingeniously produce articles to serve it, that is, to anticipate the taste and to thwart all individuality or spontaneity in it. There is, in short, what is called a "line of holiday goods," fitting, it may be supposed, the periodic line of charity. When a person receives some of these things in the blessed season of such, he is apt to be puzzled. He wants to know what they are for, what he is to do with them. If there are no "directions" on the articles, his gratitude is somewhat tempered. He has seen these nondescripts of ingenuity and expense in the shop windows, but he never expected to come into personal relations to them. He is puzzled, and he cannot escape the unpleasant feeling that commerce has put its profit-making fingers into Christmas. Such a lot of things seem to be manufactured on purpose that people may perform a duty that is expected of them in the holidays. The house is full of these impossible things; they occupy the mantelpieces, they stand about on the tottering little tables, they are ingenious, they are made for wants yet undiscovered, they tarnish, they break, they will not "work," and pretty soon they look "second-hand." Yet there must be more satisfaction in giving these articles than in receiving them, and maybe a spice of malice--not that of course, for in the holidays nearly every gift expresses at least kindly remembrance--but if you give them you do not have to live with them. But consider how full the world is of holiday goods--costly goods too--that are of no earthly use, and are not even artistic, and how short life is, and how many people actually need books and other indispensable articles, and how starved are many fine drawing-rooms, not for holiday goods, but for objects of beauty.

Christmas stands for much, and for more and more in a world that is breaking down its barriers of race and religious intolerance, and one of its chief offices has been supposed to be the teaching of men the pleasure there is in getting rid of some of their possessions for the benefit of others. But this frittering away a good instinct and tendency in conventional giving of manufactures made to suit an artificial condition is hardly in the line of developing the spirit that shares the last crust or gives to the thirsty companion in the desert the first pull at the canteen. Of course Christmas feeling is the life of trade and all that, and we will be the last to discourage any sort of giving, for one can scarcely disencumber himself of anything in his passage through this world and not be benefited; but the hint may not be thrown away that one will personally get more satisfaction out of his periodic or continual benevolence if he gives during his life the things which he wants and other people need, and reserves for a fine show in his will a collected but not selected mass of holiday goods.

CLIMATE AND HAPPINESS

The idea of the relation of climate to happiness is modern. It is probably born of the telegraph and of the possibility of rapid travel, and it is more disturbing to serenity of mind than any other. Providence had so ordered it that if we sat still in almost any region of the globe except the tropics we would have, in course of the year, almost all the kinds of climate that exist. The ancient societies did not trouble themselves about the matter; they froze or thawed, were hot or cold, as it pleased the gods. They did not think of fleeing from winter any more than from the summer solstice, and consequently they enjoyed a certain contentment of mind that is absent from modern life. We are more intelligent, and therefore more discontented and unhappy. We are always trying to escape winter when we are not trying to escape summer. We are half the time 'in transitu', flying hither and thither, craving that exact adaptation of the weather to our whimsical bodies promised only to the saints who seek a "better country." There are places, to be sure, where nature is in a sort of equilibrium, but usually those are places where we can neither make money nor spend it to our satisfaction. They lack either any stimulus to ambition or a historic association, and we soon find that the mind insists upon being cared for quite as much as the body.

How many wanderers in the past winter left comfortable homes in the United States to seek a mild climate! Did they find it in the sleet and bone-piercing cold of Paris, or anywhere in France, where the wolves were forced to come into the villages in the hope of picking up a tender child? If they traveled farther, were the railway carriages anything but refrigerators tempered by cans of cooling water? Was there a place in Europe from Spain to Greece, where the American could once be warm --really warm without effort--in or out of doors? Was it any better in divine Florence than on the chill Riviera? Northern Italy was blanketed with snow, the Apennines were white, and through the clean streets of the beautiful town a raw wind searched every nook and corner, penetrating through the thickest of English wraps, and harder to endure than ingratitude, while a frosty mist enveloped all. The traveler forgot to bring with him the contented mind of the Italian. Could he go about in a long cloak and a slouch hat, curl up in doorways out of the blast, and be content in a feeling of his own picturesqueness? Could he sit all day on the stone pavement and hold out his chilblained hand for soldi? Could he even deceive himself, in a palatial apartment with a frescoed ceiling, by an appearance of warmth in two sticks ignited by a pine cone set in an aperture in one end of the vast room, and giving out scarcely heat enough to drive the swallows from the chimney? One must be born to this sort of thing in order to enjoy it. He needs the poetic temperament which can feel in January the breath of June. The pampered American is not adapted to this kind of pleasure. He is very crude, not to say barbarous, yet in many of his tastes, but he has reached one of the desirable things in civilization, and that is a thorough appreciation of physical comfort. He has had the ingenuity to protect himself in his own climate, but when he travels he is at the mercy of customs and traditions in which the idea of physical comfort is still rudimentary. He cannot warm himself before a group of statuary, or extract heat from a canvas by Raphael, nor keep his teeth from chattering by the exquisite view from the Boboli Gardens. The cold American is insensible to art, and shivers in the presence of the warmest historical associations. It is doubtful if there is a spot in Europe where he can be ordinarily warm in winter. The world, indeed, does not care whether he is warm or not, but it is a matter of great importance to him. As he wanders from palace to palace--and he cannot escape the impression that nothing is good enough for him except a palace--he cannot think of any cottage in any hamlet in America that is not more comfortable in winter than any palace he can find. And so he is driven on in cold and weary stretches of travel to dwell among the French in Algeria, or with the Jews in Tunis, or the Moslems in Cairo. He longs for warmth as the Crusader longed for Jerusalem, but not short of Africa shall he find it. The glacial period is coming back on Europe.

The citizens of the great republic have a reputation for inordinate self-appreciation, but we are thinking that they undervalue many of the advantages their ingenuity has won. It is admitted that they are restless, and must always be seeking something that they have not at home. But aside from their ability to be warm in any part of their own country at any time of the year, where else can they travel three thousand miles on a stretch in a well-heated--too much heated--car, without change of car, without revision of tickets, without encountering a customhouse, without the necessity of stepping outdoors either for food or drink, for a library, for a bath--for any item, in short, that goes to the comfort of a civilized being? And yet we are always prating of the superior civilization of Europe. Nay, more, the traveler steps into a car--which is as comfortable as a house--in Boston, and alights from it only in the City of Mexico. In what other part of the world can that achievement in comfort and convenience be approached?

But this is not all as to climate and comfort. We have climates of all sorts within easy reach, and in quantity, both good and bad, enough to export more in fact than we need of all sorts. If heat is all we want, there are only three or four days between the zero of Maine and the 80 deg. of Florida. If New England is inhospitable and New York freezing, it is only a matter of four days to the sun and the exhilarating air of New Mexico and Arizona, and only five to the oranges and roses of that semi-tropical kingdom by the sea, Southern California. And if this does not content us, a day or two more lands us, without sea-sickness, in the land of the Aztecs, where we can live in the temperate or the tropic zone, eat strange fruits, and be reminded of Egypt and Spain and Italy, and see all the colors that the ingenuity of man has been able to give his skin. Fruits and flowers and sun in the winter-time, a climate to lounge and be happy in--all this is within easy reach, with the minimum of disturbance to our daily habits. We started out, when we turned our backs on the Old World, with the declaration that all men are free, and entitled to life, liberty, and the pursuit of an agreeable climate. We have yet to learn, it seems, that we can indulge in that pursuit best on our own continent. There is no winter climate else-where to compare with that found in our extreme Southwest or in Mexico, and the sooner we put this fact into poetry and literature, and begin to make a tradition of it, the better will it be for our peace of mind and for our children. And if the conti-nent does not satisfy us, there lie the West Indies within a few hours' sail, with all the luxuriance and geniality of the tropics. We are only half emancipated yet. We are still apt to see the world through the imagination of England, whose literature we adopted, or of Germany. To these bleak lands Italy was a paradise, and was so sung by poets who had no conception of a winter without frost. We have a winter climate of another sort from any in Europe; we have easy and comfortable access to it. The only thing we need to do now is to correct our imagination, which has been led astray. Our poets can at least do this for us by the help of a quasi-international copyright.

THE NEW FEMININE RESERVE

In times past there have been expressed desire and fear that there should be an American aristocracy, and the materials for its formation have been a good deal canvassed. In a political point of view it is of course impossible, but it has been hoped by many, and feared by more, that a social state might be created conforming somewhat to the social order in European countries. The problem has been exceedingly difficult. An aristocracy of derived rank and inherited privilege being out of the question, and an aristocracy of talent never having succeeded anywhere, because enlightenment of mind tends to liberalism and democracy, there was only left the experiment of an aristocracy of wealth. This does very well for a time, but it tends always to disintegration, and it is impossible to keep it exclusive. It was found, to use the slang of the dry-goods shops, that it would not wash, for there were liable to crowd into it at any moment those who had in fact washed for a living. An aristocracy has a slim tenure that cannot protect itself from this sort of intrusion. We have to contrive, therefore, another basis for a class (to use an un-American expression), in a sort of culture or training, which can be perpetual, and which cannot be ordered for money, like a ball costume or a livery.

Perhaps the "American Girl" may be the agency to bring this about. This charming product of the Western world has come into great prominence of late years in literature and in foreign life, and has attained a notoriety flattering or otherwise to the national pride. No institution has been better known or more marked on the Continent and in England, not excepting the tramway and the Pullman cars. Her enterprise, her daring, her freedom from conventionality, have been the theme of the novelists and the horror of the dowagers having marriageable daughters. Considered as "stock," the American Girl has been quoted high, and the alliances that she has formed with families impecunious but noble have given her eclat as belonging to a new and conquering race in the world. But the American Girl has not simply a slender figure and a fine eye and a ready tongue, she is not simply an engaging and companionable person, she has excellent common-sense, tact, and adaptability. She has at length seen in her varied European experience that it is more profitable to have social good form according to local standards than a reputation for dash and brilliancy. Consequently the American Girl of a decade ago has effaced herself. She is no longer the dazzling courageous figure. In England, in France, in Germany, in Italy, she takes, as one may say, the color of the land. She has retired behind her mother. She who formerly marched in the van of the family procession, leading them--including the panting mother--a whimsical dance, is now the timid and retiring girl, needing the protection of a chaperon on every occasion. The satirist will find no more abroad the American Girl of the old type whom he continues to describe. The knowing and fascinating creature has changed her tactics altogether. And the change has reacted on American society. The mother has come once more to the front, and even if she is obliged to own to forty-five years to the census-taker, she has again the position and the privileges of the blooming woman of thirty. Her daughters walk meekly and with downcast (if still expectant) eyes, and wait for a sign.

That this change is the deliberate work of the American Girl, no one who knows her grace and talent will deny. In foreign travel and residence she has been quick to learn her lesson. Dazzled at first by her own capacity and the opportunities of the foreign field, she took the situation by storm. But she found too often that she had a barren conquest, and that the social traditions survived her success and became a lifelong annoyance; that is to say, it was possible to subdue foreign men, but the foreign women were impregnable in their social order. The American Girl abroad is now, therefore, with rare exceptions, as carefully chaperoned and secluded as her foreign sisters.

It is not necessary to lay too much stress upon this phase of American life abroad, but the careful observer must notice its reflex action at home. The American freedom and unconventionality in the intercourse of the young of both sexes, which has been so much commented on as characteristic of American life, may not disappear, but that small section which calls itself "society" may attain a sort of aristocratic distinction by the adoption of this foreign conventionality. It is sufficient now to note this tendency, and to claim the credit of it for the wise and intelligent American Girl. It would be a pity if it were to become nationally universal, for then it would not be the aristocratic distinction of a few, and the American woman who longs for some sort of caste would be driven to some other device.

It is impossible to tell yet what form this feminine reserve and retirement will take. It is not at all likely to go so far as the Oriental seclusion of women. The American Girl would never even seemingly give up her right of initiative. If she is to stay in the background and pretend to surrender her choice to her parents, and with it all the delights of a matrimonial campaign, she will still maintain a position of observation. If she seems to be influenced at present by the French and Italian examples, we may be sure that she is too intelligent and too fond of freedom to long tolerate any system of chaperonage that she cannot control. She will find a way to modify the traditional conventionalities so as not to fetter her own free spirit. It may be her mission to show the world a social order free from the forward independence and smartness of which she has been accused, and yet relieved of the dull stiffness of the older forms. It is enough now to notice that a change is going on, due to the effect of foreign society upon American women, and to express the patriotic belief that whatever forms of etiquette she may bow to, the American Girl will still be on earth the last and best gift of God to man.

REPOSE IN ACTIVITY

What we want is repose. We take infinite trouble and go to the ends of the world to get it. That is what makes us all so restless. If we could only find a spot where we could sit down, content to let the world go by, away from the Sunday newspapers and the chronicles of an uneasy society, we think we should be happy. Perhaps such a place is Coronado Beach --that semi-tropical flower-garden by the sea. Perhaps another is the Timeo Terrace at Taormina. There, without moving, one has the most exquisite sea and shore far below him, so far that he has the feeling of domination without effort; the most picturesque crags and castle peaks; he has all classic legend under his eye without the trouble of reading, and mediaeval romance as well; ruins from the time of Theocritus to Freeman, with no responsibility of describing them; and one of the loveliest and most majestic of snow mountains, never twice the same in light and shade, entirely revealed and satisfactory from base to summit, with no self or otherwise imposed duty of climbing it. Here are most of the elements of peace and calm spirit. And the town itself is quite dead, utterly exhausted after a turbulent struggle of twenty-five hundred years, its poor inhabitants living along only from habit. The only new things in it--the two caravansaries of the traveler--are a hotel and a cemetery. One might end his days here in serene retrospection, and more cheaply than in other places of fewer attractions, for it is all Past and no Future. Probably, therefore, it would not suit the American, whose imagination does not work so easily backward as forward, and who prefers to build his own nest rather than settle in anybody else's rookery. Perhaps the American deceives himself when he says he wants repose; what he wants is perpetual activity and change; his peace of mind is postponed until he can get it in his own way. It is in feeling that he is a part of growth and not of decay. Foreigners are fond of writing essays upon American traits and characteristics. They touch mostly on surface indications. What really distinguishes the American from all others--for all peoples like more or less to roam, and the English of all others are globe-trotters--is not so much his restlessness as his entire accord with the spirit of "go-ahead," the result of his absolute breaking with the Past. He can repose only in the midst of intense activity. He can sit down quietly in a town that is growing rapidly; but if it stands still, he is impelled to move his rocking-chair to one more lively. He wants the world to move, and to move unencumbered; and Europe seems to him to carry too much baggage. The American is simply the most modern of men, one who has thrown away the impedimenta of tradition. The world never saw such a spectacle before, so vast a territory informed with one uniform spirit of energy and progress, and people tumbling into it from all the world, eager for the fair field and free opportunity. The American delights in it; in Europe he misses the swing and "go" of the new life.

This large explanation may not account for the summer restlessness that overtakes nearly everybody. We are the annual victims of the delusion that there exists somewhere the ideal spot where manners are simple, and milk is pure, and lodging is cheap, where we shall fall at once into content. We never do. For content consists not in having all we want, nor, in not wanting everything, nor in being unable to get what we want, but in not wanting that we can get. In our summer flittings we carry our wants with us to places where they cannot be gratified. A few people have discovered that repose can be had at home, but this discovery is too unfashionable to find favor; we have no rest except in moving about. Looked at superficially, it seems curious that the American is, as a rule, the only person who does not emigrate. The fact is that he can go nowhere else where life is so uneasy, and where, consequently, he would have so little of his sort of repose. To put him in another country would be like putting a nineteenth-century man back into the eighteenth century. The American wants to be at the head of the procession (as he fancies he is), where he can hear the band play, and be the first to see the fireworks of the new era. He thinks that he occupies an advanced station of observation, from which his telescope can sweep the horizon for anything new. And with some reason he thinks so; for not seldom he takes up a foreign idea and tires of it before it is current elsewhere. More than one great writer of England had his first popular recognition in America. Even this season the Saturday Review is struggling with Ibsen, while

Boston, having had that disease, has probably gone on to some other fad.

Far be it from us to praise the American for his lack of repose; it is enough to attempt to account for it. But from the social, or rather society, point of view, the subject has a disquieting aspect. If the American young man and young woman get it into their heads that repose, especially of manner, is the correct thing, they will go in for it in a way to astonish the world. The late cultivation of idiocy by the American dude was unique. He carried it to an extreme impossible to the youth of any nation less "gifted." And if the American girl goes in seriously for "repose," she will be able to give odds to any modern languidity or to any ancient marble. If what is wanted in society is cold hauteur and languid superciliousness or lofty immobility, we are confident that with a little practice she can sit stiller, and look more impassive, and move with less motion, than any other created woman. We have that confidence in her ability and adaptability. It is a question whether it is worth while to do this; to sacrifice the vivacity and charm native to her, and the natural impulsiveness and generous gift of herself which belong to a new race in a new land, which is walking always towards the sunrise.

In fine, although so much is said of the American lack of repose, is it not best for the American to be content to be himself, and let the critics adapt themselves or not, as they choose, to a new phenomenon?

Let us stick a philosophic name to it, and call it repose in activity. The American might take the candid advice given by one friend to another, who complained that it was so difficult to get into the right frame of mind. "The best thing you can do," he said, "is to frame your mind and hang it up."

WOMEN--IDEAL AND REAL

We have not by any means got to the bottom of Realism. It matters very little what the novelists and critics say about it--what it is and what it is not; the attitude of society towards it is the important thing. Even if the critic could prove that nature and art are the same thing, and that the fiction which is Real is only a copy of nature, or if another should prove that Reality is only to be found in the Ideal, little would be gained. Literature is well enough in its place, art is an agreeable pastime, and it is right that society should take up either in seasons when lawn-tennis and polo are impracticable and afternoon teas become flavorless; but the question that society is or should be interested in is whether the young woman of the future--upon whose formation all our social hopes depend--is going to shape herself by a Realistic or an Ideal standard. It should be said in parenthesis that the young woman of the passing period has inclined towards Realism in manner and speech, if not in dress, affecting a sort of frank return to the easy-going ways of nature itself, even to the adoption of the language of the stock exchange, the race-course, and the clubs--an offering of herself on the altar of good-fellowship, with the view, no doubt, of making life more agreeable to the opposite sex, forgetting the fact that men fall in love always, or used to in the days when they could afford that luxury, with an ideal woman, or if not with an ideal woman, with one whom they idealize. And at this same time the world is full of doubts and questionings as to whether marriage is a failure. Have these questionings anything to do with the increasing Realism of women, and a consequent loss of ideals?

Of course the reader sees that the difficulty in considering this subject is whether woman is to be estimated as a work of nature or of art. And here comes in the everlasting question of what is the highest beauty, and what is most to be desired.

The Greek artists, it seems to be well established, never used a model, as our artists almost invariably do, in their plastic and pictorial creations. The antique Greek statues, or their copies, which give us the highest conceptions of feminine charm and manly beauty, were made after no woman, or man born of woman, but were creations of the ideal raised to the highest conception by the passionate love and long study of nature, but never by faithful copying of it. The Romans copied the Greek art. The Greek in his best days created the ideal figure, which we love to accept as nature. Generation after generation the Greek learned to draw and learned to observe, until he was able to transmute his knowledge into the forms of grace and beauty which satisfy us as nature at her best; just as the novelist trains all his powers by the observation of life until he is able to transmute all the raw material into a creation of fiction which satisfies us. We may be sure that if the Greek artist had employed the service of models in his studio, his art would have been merely a passing phase in human history. But as it is, the world has ever since been in love with his ideal woman, and still believes in her possibility.

Now the young woman of today should not be deceived into the notion of a preferable Realistic development because the novelist of today gets her to sit to him as his model. This may be no certain indication that she is either good art or good nature. Indeed she may be quite drifting away from the ideal that a woman ought to aim at if we are to have a society that is not always tending into a realistic vulgarity and commonplace. It is perfectly true that a woman is her own excuse for being, and in a way she is doing enough for the world by simply being a woman. It is difficult to rouse her to any sense of her duty as a standard of aspiration. And it is difficult to explain exactly what it is that she is to do. If she asks if she is expected to be a model woman, the reply must be that the world does not much hanker after what--is called the "model woman." It seems to be more a matter of tendency than anything else. Is she sagging towards Realism or rising towards Idealism? Is she content to be the woman that some of the novelists, and some of the painters also, say she is, or would she prefer to approach that ideal which all the world loves? It is a question of standards.

It is natural that in these days, when the approved gospel is that it is better to be dead than not to be Real, society should try to approach nature by the way of the materialistically ignoble, and even go such a pace of Realism as literature finds it difficult to keep up with; but it is doubtful if the young woman will get around to any desirable state of nature by this route. We may not be able to explain why servile imitation of nature degrades art and degrades woman, but both deteriorate without an ideal so high that there is no earthly model for it. Would you like to marry, perhaps, a Greek statue? says the justly contemptuous critic.

Not at all, at least not a Roman copy of one. But it would be better to marry a woman who would rather be like a Greek statue than like some of these figures, without even an idea for clothing, which are lying about on green banks in our spring exhibitions.

THE ART OF IDLENESS

Idleness seems to be the last accomplishment of civilization. To be idle gracefully and contentedly and picturesquely is an art. It is one in which the Americans, who do so many things well, do not excel. They have made the excuse that they have not time, or, if they have leisure, that their temperament and nervous organization do not permit it. This excuse will pass for a while, for we are a new people, and probably we are more highly and sensitively organized than any other nation--at least the physiologists say so; but the excuse seems more and more inadequate as we accumulate wealth, and consequently have leisure. We shall not criticise the American colonies in Paris and Rome and Florence, and in other Continental places where they congregate. They know whether they are restless or contented, and what examples they set to the peoples who get their ideas of republican simplicity and virtue from the Americans who sojourn among them. They know whether with all their leisure they get placidity of mind and the real rest which the older nations have learned to enjoy. It may not be the most desirable thing for a human being to be idle, but if he will be, he should be so in a creditable manner, and with some enjoyment to himself. It is no slander to say that we in America have not yet found out the secret of this. Perhaps we shall not until our energies are spent and we are in a state of decay. At present we put as much energy into our pleasure as into our work, for it is inbred in us that laziness is a sin. This is the Puritan idea, and it must be said for it that in our experience virtue and idleness are not commonly companions. But this does not go to the bottom of the matter.

The Italians are industrious; they are compelled to be in order to pay their taxes for the army and navy and get macaroni enough to live on. But see what a long civilization has done for them. They have the manner of laziness, they have the air of leisure, they have worn off the angular corners of existence, and unconsciously their life is picturesque and enjoyable. Those among them who have money take their pleasure simply and with the least expense of physical energy. Those who have not money do the same thing. This basis of existence is calm and unexaggerated; life is reckoned by centimes, not by dollars. What an ideal place is Venice! It is not only the most picturesque city in the world, rich in all that art can invent to please the eye, but how calm it is! The vivacity which entertains the traveler is all on the surface. The nobleman in his palace if there be any palace that is not turned into a hotel, or a magazine of curiosities, or a municipal office--can live on a diet that would make an American workman strike, simply because he has learned to float through life; and the laborer is equally happy on little because he has learned to wait without much labor. The gliding, easy motion of the gondola expresses the whole situation; and the gondolier who with consummate skill urges his dreamy bark amid the throng and in the tortuous canals for an hour or two, and then sleeps in the sun, is a type of that rest in labor which we do not attain. What happiness there is in a dish of polenta, or of a few fried fish, in a cup of coffee, and in one of those apologies for cigars which the government furnishes, dear at a cent--the cigar with a straw in it, as if it were a julep, which it needs five minutes to ignite, and then will furnish occupation for a whole evening! Is it a hard lot, that of the fishermen and the mariners of the Adriatic? The lights are burning all night long in a cafe on the Riva del Schiavoni, and the sailors and idlers of the shore sit there jabbering and singing and trying their voices in lusty hallooing till the morning light begins to make the lagoon opalescent. The traveler who lodges near cannot sleep, but no more can the sailors, who steal away in the dawn, wafted by painted sails. In the heat of the day, when the fish will not bite, comes the siesta. Why should the royal night be wasted in slumber? The shore of the Riva, the Grand Canal, the islands, gleam with twinkling lamps; the dark boats glide along with a star in the prow, bearing youth and beauty and sin and ugliness, all alike softened by the shadows; the electric lights from the shores and the huge steamers shoot gleams on towers and facades; the moon wades among the fleecy clouds; here and there a barge with colored globes of light carries a band of singing men and women and players on the mandolin and the fiddle, and from every side the songs of Italy, pathetic in their worn gayety, float to the entranced ears of those who lean from balconies, or lounge in gondolas and listen with hearts made a little heavy and wistful with so much beauty.

Can any one float in such scenes and be so contentedly idle anywhere in our happy land? Have we learned yet the simple art of easy enjoyment? Can we buy it with money quickly, or is it a grace that comes only with long civilization? Italy, for instance, is full of accumulated wealth, of art, even of ostentation and display, and the new generation probably have lost the power to conceive, if not the skill to execute, the great works which excite our admiration. Nothing can be much more meretricious than its modern art, when anything is produced that is not an exact copy of something created when there was genius there. But in one respect the Italians have entered into the fruits of the ages of trial and of failure, and that, is the capacity of being idle with much money or with none, and getting day by day their pay for the bother of living in this world. It seems a difficult lesson for us to learn in country or city. Alas! when we have learned it shall we not want to emigrate, as so many of the Italians do? Some philosophers say that men were not created to be happy. Perhaps they were not intended to be idle.

IS THERE ANY CONVERSATION

Is there any such thing as conversation? It is a delicate subject to touch, because many people understand conversation to be talk; not the exchange of ideas, but of words; and we would not like to say anything to increase the flow of the latter. We read of times and salons in which real conversation existed, held by men and women. Are they altogether in the past? We believe that men do sometimes converse. Do women ever? Perhaps so. In those hours sacred to the relaxation of undress and the back hair, in the upper penetralia of the household, where two or three or six are gathered together on and about the cushioned frame intended for repose, do they converse, or indulge in that sort of chat from which not one idea is carried away? No one reports, fortunately, and we do not know. But do all the women like this method of spending hour after hour, day after day-indeed, a lifetime? Is it invigorating, even restful? Think of the talk this past summer, the rivers and oceans of it, on piazzas and galleries in the warm evenings or the fresher mornings, in private houses, on hotel verandas, in the shade of thousands of cottages by the sea and in the hills! As you recall it, what was it all about? Was the mind in a vapid condition after an evening of it? And there is so much to read, and so much to think about, and the world is so interesting, if you do think about it, and nearly every person has some peculiarity of mind that would be worth study if you could only get at it! It is really, we repeat, such an interesting world, and most people get so little out of it. Now there is the conversation of hens, when the hens are busy and not self-conscious; there is something fascinating about it, because the imagination may invest it with a recondite and spicy meaning; but the common talk of people! We infer sometimes that the hens are not saying anything, because they do not read, and consequently their minds are empty. And perhaps we are right. As to conversation, there is no use in sending the bucket into the well when the well is dry-

-it only makes a rattling of windlass and chain. We do not wish to be understood to be an enemy of the light traffic of human speech. Deliver us from the didactic and the everlastingly improving style of thing! Conversation, in order to be good, and intellectually inspiring, and spiritually restful, need not always be serious. It must be alert and intelligent, and mean more by its suggestions and allusions than is said. There is the light touch-and-go play about topics more or less profound that is as agreeable as heat-lightning in a sultry evening. Why may not a person express the whims and vagaries of a lambent mind (if he can get a lambent mind) without being hauled up short for it, and plunged into a heated dispute? In the freedom of real conversation the mind throws out half-thoughts, paradoxes, for which a man is not to be held strictly responsible to the very roots of his being, and which need to be caught up and played with in the same tentative spirit. The dispute and the hot argument are usually the bane of conversation and the death of originality. We like to express a notion, a fancy, without being called upon to defend it, then and there, in all its possible consequences, as if it were to be an article in a creed or a plank in a platform. Must we be always either vapid or serious?

We have been obliged to take notice of the extraordinary tendency of American women to cultivation, to the improvement of the mind, by means of reading, clubs, and other intellectual exercises, and to acknowledge that they are leaving the men behind; that is, the men not in the so-called professions. Is this intellectualization beginning to show in the conversation of women when they are together, say in the hours of relaxation in the penetralia spoken of, or in general society? Is there less talk about the fashion of dress, and the dearness or cheapness of materials, and about servants, and the ways of the inchoate citizen called the baby, and the infinitely little details of the private life of other people? Is it true that if a group of men are talking, say about politics, or robust business, or literature, and they are joined by women (whose company is always welcome), the conversation is pretty sure to take a lower mental plane, to become more personal, more frivolous, accommodating itself to quite a different range? Do the well-read, thoughtful women, however beautiful and brilliant and capable of the gayest persiflage, prefer to talk with men, to listen to the conversation of men, rather than to converse with or listen to their own sex? If this is true, why is it? Women, as a rule, in "society" at any rate, have more leisure than men. In the facilities and felicities of speech they commonly excel men, and usually they have more of that vivacious dramatic power which is called "setting out a thing to the life." With all these advantages, and all the world open to them in newspapers and in books, they ought to be the leaders and stimulators of the best conversation. With them it should never drop down to the too-common flatness and banality. Women have made this world one of the most beautiful places of residence to be conceived. They might make it one of the most interesting.

THE TALL GIRL

It is the fashion for girls to be tall. This is much more than saying that tall girls are the fashion. It means not only that the tall girl has come in, but that girls are tall, and are becoming tall, because it is the fashion, and because there is a demand for that sort of girl. There is no hint of stoutness, indeed the willowy pattern is preferred, but neither is leanness suggested; the women of the period have got hold of the poet's idea, "tall and most divinely fair," and are living up to it. Perhaps this change in fashion is more noticeable in England and on the Continent than in America, but that may be because there is less room for change in America, our girls being always of an aspiring turn. Very marked the phenomenon is in England; on the street, at any concert or reception, the number of tall girls is so large as to occasion remark, especially among the young girls just coming into the conspicuousness of womanhood. The tendency of the new generation is towards unusual height and gracious slimness. The situation would be embarrassing to thousands of men who have been too busy to think about growing upward, were it not for the fact that the tall girl, who must be looked up to, is almost invariably benignant, and bears her height with a sweet timidity that disarms fear. Besides, the tall girl has now come on in such force that confidence is infused into the growing army, and there is a sense of support in this survival of the tallest that is very encouraging to the young.

Many theories have been put forward to account for this phenomenon. It is known that delicate plants in dark places struggle up towards the light in a frail slenderness, and it is said that in England, which seems to have increasing cloudiness, and in the capital more and more months of deeper darkness and blackness, it is natural that the British girl should grow towards the light. But this is a fanciful view of the case, for it cannot be proved that English men have proportionally increased their stature. The English man has always seemed big to the Continental peoples, partly because objects generally take on gigantic dimensions when seen through a fog. Another theory, which has much more to commend it, is that the increased height of women is due to the aesthetic movement, which has now spent its force, but has left certain results, especially in the change of the taste in colors. The woman of the aesthetic artist was nearly always tall, usually willowy, not to say undulating and serpentine. These forms of feminine loveliness and command-ing height have been for many years before the eyes of the women of England in paintings and drawings, and it is unavoidable that this pattern should not have its effect upon the new and plastic generation. Never has there been another genera-tion so open to new ideas; and if the ideal of womanhood held up was that of length and gracious slenderness, it would be very odd if women should not aspire to it. We know very well the influence that the heroines of the novelists have had from time to time upon the women of a given period. The heroine of Scott was, no doubt, once common in society--the delicate creature who promptly fainted on the remi-niscence of the scent of a rose, but could stand any amount of dragging by the hair through underground passages, and midnight rides on lonely moors behind mailed and black-mantled knights, and a run or two of hair-removing typhoid fever, and come out at the end of the story as fresh as a daisy. She could not be found now, so changed are the requirements of fiction. We may assume, too, that the full-blown aesthetic girl of that recent period--the girl all soul and faded harmonies--would be hard to find, but the fascination of the height and slenderness of that girl remains something more than a tradition, and is, no doubt, to some extent copied by the maiden just coming into her kingdom.

Those who would belittle this matter may say that the appearance of which we speak is due largely to the fashion of dress--the long unbroken lines which add to the height and encourage the appearance of slenderness. But this argument gives away the case. Why do women wear the present fascinating gowns, in which the lithe figure is suggested in all its womanly dignity? In order that they may appear to be tall. That is to say, because it is the fashion to be tall; women born in the mode are tall, and those caught in a hereditary shortness endeavor to conform to the stat-ure of the come and coming woman.

There is another theory, that must be put forward with some hesitation, for the so-called emancipation of woman is a delicate subject to deal with, for while all the sex doubtless feel the impulse of the new time, there are still many who indignantly reject the implication in the struggle for the rights of women. To say, therefore, that women are becoming tall as a part of their outfit for taking the place of men in this world would be to many an affront, so that this theory can only be suggested. Yet probably physiology would bear us out in saying that the truly emancipated woman, taking at last the place in affairs which men have flown in the face of Providence by denying her, would be likely to expand physically as well as mentally, and that as she is beginning to look down upon man intellectually, she is likely to have a corresponding physical standard.

Seriously, however, none of these theories are altogether satisfactory, and we are inclined to seek, as is best in all cases, the simplest explanation. Women are tall and becoming tall simply because it is the fashion, and that statement never needs nor is capable of any explanation. Awhile ago it was the fashion to be petite and arch; it is now the fashion to be tall and gracious, and nothing more can be said about it. Of course the reader, who is usually inclined to find the facetious side of any grave topic, has already thought of the application of the self-denying hymn, that man wants but little here below, and wants that little long; but this may be only a passing sigh of the period. We are far from expressing any preference for tall women over short women. There are creative moods of the fancy when each seems the better. We can only chronicle, but never create.

THE DEADLY DIARY

Many people regard the keeping of a diary as a meritorious occupation. The young are urged to take up this cross; it is supposed to benefit girls especially. Whether women should do it is to some minds not an open question, although there is on record the case of the Frenchman who tried to shoot himself when he heard that his wife was keeping a diary. This intention of suicide may have arisen from the fear that his wife was keeping a record of his own peccadilloes rather than of her own thoughts and emotions. Or it may have been from the fear that she was putting down those little conjugal remarks which the husband always dislikes to have thrown up to him, and which a woman can usually quote accurately, it may be for years, it may be forever, without the help of a diary. So we can appreciate without approving the terror of the Frenchman at living on and on in the same house with a growing diary. For it is not simply that this little book of judgment is there in black and white, but that the maker of it is increasing her power of minute observation and analytic expression. In discussing the question whether a woman should keep a diary it is understood that it is not a mere memorandum of events and engagements, such as both men and women of business and affairs necessarily keep, but the daily record which sets down feelings, emotions, and impressions, and criticises people and records opinions. But this is a question that applies to men as well as to women.

It has been assumed that the diary serves two good purposes: it is a disciplinary exercise for the keeper of it, and perhaps a moral guide; and it has great historical value. As to the first, it may be helpful to order, method, discipline, and it may be an indulgence of spleen, whims, and unwholesome criticism and conceit. The habit of saying right out what you think of everybody is not a good one, and the record of such opinions and impressions, while it is not so mischievous to the public as talking may be, is harmful to the recorder. And when we come to the historical value of the diary, we confess to a growing suspicion of it. It is such a deadly weapon when it comes to light after the passage of years. It has an authority which the spoken words of its keeper never had. It is 'ex parte', and it cannot be cross-examined. The supposition is that being contemporaneous with the events spoken of, it must be true, and that it is an honest record. Now, as a matter of fact, we doubt if people are any more honest as to themselves or others in a diary than out of it; and rumors, reported facts, and impressions set down daily in the heat and haste of the prejudicial hour are about as likely to be wrong as right. Two diaries of the same events rarely agree. And in turning over an old diary we never know what to allow for the personal equation. The diary is greatly relied on by the writers of history, but it is doubtful if there is any such liar in the world, even when the keeper of it is honest. It is certain to be partisan, and more liable to be misinformed than a newspaper, which exercises some care in view of immediate publicity. The writer happens to know of two diaries which record, on the testimony of eye-witnesses, the circumstances of the last hours of Garfield, and they differ utterly in essential particulars. One of these may turn up fifty years from now, and be accepted as true. An infinite amount of gossip goes into diaries about men and women that would not stand the test of a moment's contemporary publication. But by-and-by it may all be used to smirch or brighten unjustly some one's character. Suppose a man in the Army of the Potomac had recorded daily all his opinions of men and events. Reading it over now, with more light and a juster knowledge of character and of measures, is it not probable that he would find it a tissue of misconceptions? Few things are actually what they seem today; they are colored both by misapprehensions and by moods. If a man writes a letter or makes report of an occurrence for immediate publication, subject to universal criticism, there is some restraint on him. In his private letter, or diary especially, he is apt to set down what comes into his head at the moment, often without much effort at verification.

We have been led to this disquisition into the fundamental nature of this private record by the question put to us, whether it is a good plan for a woman to keep a diary. Speaking generally, the diary has become a sort of fetich, the authority of which ought to be overthrown. It is fearful to think how our characters are probably being lied away by innumerable pen scratches in secret repositories, which may some day come to light as unimpeachable witnesses. The reader knows that he is not the sort of man which the diarist jotted him down to be in a single inter-view. The diary may be a good thing for self-education, if the keeper could insure its destruction. The mental habit of diarizing may have some value, even when it sets undue importance upon trifles. We confess that, never having seen a woman's private diary (except those that have been published), we do not share the popular impression as to their tenuity implied in the question put to us. Taking it for granted that they are full of noble thoughts and beautiful imaginings, we doubt whether the time spent on them could not be better employed in acquiring knowledge or taking exercise. For the diary forgotten and left to the next generation may be as dangerous as dynamite.

THE WHISTLING GIRL

The wisdom of our ancestors packed away in proverbial sayings may always be a little suspected. We have a vague respect for a popular proverb, as embodying folk-experience, and expressing not the wit of one, but the common thought of a race. We accept the saying unquestioning, as a sort of inspiration out of the air, true because nobody has challenged it for ages, and probably for the same reason that we try to see the new moon over our left shoulder. Very likely the musty saying was the product of the average ignorance of an unenlightened time, and ought not to have the respect of a scientific and traveled people. In fact it will be found that a large proportion of the proverbial sayings which we glibly use are fallacies based on a very limited experience of the world, and probably were set afloat by the idiocy or prejudice of one person. To examine one of them is enough for our present purpose.

"Whistling girls and crowing hens   Always come to some bad ends."

It would be interesting to know the origin of this proverb, because it is still much relied on as evincing a deep knowledge of human nature, and as an argument against change, that is to say, in this case, against progress. It would seem to have been made by a man, conservative, perhaps malevolent, who had no appreciation of a hen, and a conservatively poor opinion of woman. His idea was to keep woman in her place--a good idea when not carried too far--but he did not know what her place is, and he wanted to put a sort of restraint upon her emancipation by coupling her with an emancipated hen. He therefore launched this shaft of ridicule, and got it to pass as an arrow of wisdom shot out of a popular experience in remote ages.

In the first place, it is not true, and probably never was true even when hens were at their lowest. We doubts its Sanscrit antiquity. It is perhaps of Puritan origin, and rhymed in New England. It is false as to the hen. A crowing hen was always an object of interest and distinction; she was pointed out to visitors; the owner was proud of her accomplishment, he was naturally likely to preserve her life, and especially if she could lay. A hen that can lay and crow is a 'rara avis'. And it should be parenthetically said here that the hen who can crow and cannot lay is not a good example for woman. The crowing hen was of more value than the silent hen, provided she crowed with discretion; and she was likely to be a favorite, and not at all to come to some bad end. Except, indeed, where the proverb tended to work its own fulfillment. And this is the regrettable side of most proverbs of an ill-nature, that they do help to work the evil they predict. Some foolish boy, who had heard this proverb, and was sent out to the hen-coop in the evening to slay for the Thanksgiving feast, thought he was a justifiable little providence in wringing the neck of the crowing hen, because it was proper (according to the saying) that she should come to some bad end. And as years went on, and that kind of boy increased and got to be a man, it became a fixed idea to kill the amusing, interesting, spirited, emancipated hen, and naturally the barn-yard became tamer and tamer, the production of crowing hens was discouraged (the wise old hens laid no eggs with a crow in them, according to the well-known principle of heredity), and the man who had in his youth exterminated the hen of progress actually went about quoting that false couplet as an argument against the higher education of woman.

As a matter of fact, also, the couplet is not true about woman; whether it ought to be true is an ethical question that will not be considered here. The whistling girl does not commonly come to a bad end. Quite as often as any other girl she learns to whistle a cradle song, low and sweet and charming, to the young voter in the cradle. She is a girl of spirit, of independence of character, of dash and flavor; and as to lips, why, you must have some sort of presentable lips to whistle; thin ones will not. The whistling girl does not come to a bad end at all (if marriage is still considered a good occupation), except a cloud may be thrown upon her exuberant young life by this rascally proverb. Even if she walks the lonely road of life, she has this advantage, that she can whistle to keep her courage up. But in a larger sense, one that this practical age can understand, it is not true that the whistling girl comes to a bad end. Whistling pays. It has brought her money; it has blown her name about the listening world. Scarcely has a non-whistling woman been more famous. She has set aside the adage. She has done so much towards the emancipation of her sex from the prejudice created by an ill-natured proverb which never had root in fact.

But has the whistling woman come to stay? Is it well for woman to whistle? Are the majority of women likely to be whistlers? These are serious questions, not to be taken up in a light manner at the end of a grave paper. Will woman ever learn to throw a stone? There it is. The future is inscrutable. We only know that whereas they did not whistle with approval, now they do; the prejudice of generations gradually melts away. And woman's destiny is not linked with that of the hen, nor to be controlled by a proverb--perhaps not by anything.

BORN OLD AND RICH

We have been remiss in not proposing a remedy for our present social and economic condition. Looking backward, we see this. The scheme may not be practical, any more than the Utopian plans that have been put forward, but it is radical and interesting, and requires, as the other schemes do, a total change in human nature (which may be a good thing to bring about), and a general recasting of the conditions of life. This is and should be no objection to a socialistic scheme. Surface measures will not avail. The suggestion for a minor alleviation of inequality, which seems to have been acted on, namely, that women should propose, has not had the desired effect if it is true, as reported, that the eligible young men are taking to the woods. The workings of such a measure are as impossible to predict in advance as the operation of the McKinley tariff. It might be well to legislate that people should be born equal (including equal privileges of the sexes), but the practical difficulty is to keep them equal. Life is wrong somehow. Some are born rich and some are born poor, and this inequality makes misery, and then some lose their possessions, which others get hold of, and that makes more misery. We can put our fingers on the two great evils of life as it now is: the first is poverty; and the second is infirmity, which is the accompaniment of increasing years. Poverty, which is only the unequal distribution of things desired, makes strife, and is the opportunity of lawyers; and infirmity is the excuse for doctors. Think what the world would be without lawyers and doctors!

We are all born young, and most of us are born poor. Youth is delightful, but we are always getting away from it. How different it would be if we were always going towards it! Poverty is unpleasant, and the great struggle of life is to get rid of it; but it is the common fortune that in proportion as wealth is attained the capacity of enjoying it departs. It seems, therefore, that our life is wrong end first. The remedy suggested is that men should be born rich and old. Instead of the necessity of making a fortune, which is of less and less value as death approaches, we should have only the privilege of spending it, and it would have its natural end in the cradle, in which we should be rocked into eternal sleep. Born old, one would, of course, inherit experience, so that wealth could be made to contribute to happiness, and each day, instead of lessening the natural powers and increasing infirmities, would bring new vigor and capacity of enjoyment. It would be going from winter to autumn, from autumn to summer, from summer to spring. The joy of a life without care as to ways and means, and every morning refitted with the pulsations of increasing youth, it is almost impossible to imagine. Of course this scheme has difficulties on the face of it. The allotting of the measure of wealth would not be difficult to the socialists, because they would insist that every person should be born with an equal amount of property. What this should be would depend upon the length of life; and how should this be arrived at? The insurance companies might agree, but no one else would admit that he belongs in the average. Naturally the Biblical limit of threescore and ten suggests itself; but human nature is very queer. With the plain fact before them that the average life of man is less than thirty-four years, few would be willing, if the choice were offered, to compromise on seventy. Everybody has a hope of going beyond that, so that if seventy were proposed as the year at birth, there would no doubt be as much dissatisfaction as there is at the present loose arrangement. Science would step in, and demonstrate that there is no reason why, with proper care of the system, it should not run a hundred years. It is improbable, then, that the majority could be induced to vote for the limit of seventy years, or to exchange the exciting uncertainty of adding a little to the period which must be accompanied by the weight of the grasshopper, for the certainty of only seventy years in this much-abused world.

But suppose a limit to be agreed on, and the rich old man and the rich old woman (never now too old to marry) to start on their career towards youth and poverty. The imagination kindles at the idea. The money would hold out just as long as life lasted, and though it would all be going downhill, as it were, what a charming descent, without struggle, and with only the lessening infirmities that belong to decreasing age! There would be no second childhood, only the innocence and elasticity of the first. It all seems very fair, but we must not forget that this is a mortal world, and that it is liable to various accidents. Who, for instance, could be sure that he would grow young gracefully? There would be the constant need of fighting the hot tempers and impulses of youth, growing more and more instead of less and less unreasonable. And then, how many would reach youth? More than half, of course, would be cut off in their prime, and be more and more liable to go as they fell back into the pitfalls and errors of childhood. Would people grow young together even as harmoniously as they grow old together? It would be a pretty sight, that of the few who descended into the cradle together, but this inversion of life would not escape the woes of mortality. And there are other considerations, unless it should turn out that a universal tax on land should absolutely change human nature. There are some who would be as idle and spendthrift going towards youth as they now are going away from it, and perhaps more, so that half the race on coming to immaturity would be in child asylums. And then others who would be stingy and greedy and avaricious, and not properly spend their allotted fortune. And we should have the anomaly, which is so distasteful to the reformer now, of rich babies. A few babies inordinately rich, and the rest in asylums.

Still, the plan has more to recommend it than most others for removing poverty and equalizing conditions. We should all start rich, and the dying off of those who would never attain youth would amply provide fortunes for those born old. Crime would be less also; for while there would, doubtless, be some old sinners, the criminal class, which is very largely under thirty, would be much smaller than it is now. Juvenile depravity would proportionally disappear, as not more people would reach non-age than now reach over-age. And the great advantage of the scheme, one that would indeed transform the world, is that women would always be growing younger.

THE "OLD SOLDIER"

The "old soldier" is beginning to outline himself upon the public mind as a distant character in American life. Literature has not yet got hold of him, and perhaps his evolution is not far enough advanced to make him as serviceable as the soldier of the Republic and the Empire, the relic of the Old Guard, was to Hugo and Balzac, the trooper of Italy and Egypt, the maimed hero of Borodino and Waterloo, who expected again the coming of the Little Corporal. It takes time to develop a character, and to throw the glamour of romance over what may be essentially commonplace. A quarter of a century has not sufficed to separate the great body of the surviving volunteers in the war for the Union from the body of American citizens, notwithstanding the organization of the Grand Army of the Republic, the encampments, the annual reunions, and the distinction of pensions, and the segregation in Soldiers' Homes. The "old soldier" slowly eliminates himself from the mass, and begins to take, and to make us take, a romantic view of his career. There was one event in his life, and his personality in it looms larger and larger as he recedes from it. The heroic sacrifice of it does not diminish, as it should not, in our estimation, and he helps us to keep glowing a lively sense of it. The past centres about him and his great achievement, and the whole of life is seen in the light of it. In his retreat in the Home, and in his wandering from one Home to another, he ruminates on it, he talks of it; he separates himself from the rest of mankind by a broad distinction, and his point of view of life becomes as original as it is interesting. In the Homes the battered veterans speak mainly of one thing; and in the monotony of their spent lives develop whimseys and rights and wrongs, patriotic ardors and criticisms on their singular fate, which are original in their character in our society. It is in human nature to like rest but not restriction, bounty but not charity, and the tired heroes of the war grow restless, though every physical want is supplied. They have a fancy that they would like to see again the homes of their youth, the farmhouse in the hills, the cottage in the river valley, the lonesome house on the wide prairie, the street that ran down to the wharf where the fishing-smacks lay, to see again the friends whom they left there, and perhaps to take up the occupations that were laid down when they seized the musket in 1861. Alas! it is not their home anymore; the friends are no longer there; and what chance is there of occupation for a man who is now feeble in body and who has the habit of campaigning? This generation has passed on to other things. It looks upon the hero as an illustration in the story of the war, which it reads like history. The veteran starts out from the shelter of the Home. One evening, towards sunset, the comfortable citizen, taking the mild air on his piazza, sees an interesting figure approach. Its dress is half military, half that of the wanderer whose attention to his personal appearance is only spasmodic.

The veteran gives the military salute, he holds himself erect, almost too erect, and his speech is voluble and florid. It is a delightful evening; it seems to be a good growing-time; the country looks prosperous. He is sorry to be any trouble or interruption, but the fact is--yes, he is on his way to his old home in Vermont; it seems like he would like to taste some home cooking again, and sit in the old orchard, and perhaps lay his bones, what is left of them, in the burying-ground on the hill. He pulls out his well-worn papers as he talks; there is the honorable discharge, the permit of the Home, and the pension. Yes, Uncle Sam is generous; it is the most generous government God ever made, and he would willingly fight for it again. Thirty dollars a month, that is what he has; he is not a beggar; he wants for nothing. But the pension is not payable till the end of the month. It is entirely his own obligation, his own fault; he can fight, but he cannot lie, and nobody is to blame but himself; but last night he fell in with some old comrades at Southdown, and, well, you know how it is. He had plenty of money when he left the Home, and he is not asking for anything now, but if he had a few dollars for his railroad fare to the next city, he could walk the rest of the way. Wounded? Well, if I stood out here against the light you could just see through me, that's all. Bullets? It's no use to try to get 'em out. But, sir, I'm not complaining. It had to be done; the country had to be saved; and I'd do it again if it were necessary. Had any hot fights? Sir, I was at Gettysburg! The veteran straightens up, and his eyes flash as if he saw again that sanguinary field. Off goes the citizen's hat. Children, come out here; here is one of the soldiers of Gettys-burg! Yes, sir; and this knee--you see I can't bend it much--got stiffened at Chicka-mauga; and this scratch here in the neck was from a bullet at Gaines Mill; and this here, sir--thumping his chest--you notice I don't dare to cough much --after the explosion of a shell at Petersburg I found myself lying on my-back, and the only one of my squad who was not killed outright. Was it the imagination of the citizen or of the soldier that gave the impression that the hero had been in the forefront of every important action of the war? Well, it doesn't matter much. The citizen was sitting there under his own vine, the comfortable citizen of a free republic, because of the wounds in this cheerful and imaginative old wanderer. There, that is enough, sir, quite enough. I am no beggar. I thought perhaps you had heard of the Ninth Vermont. Woods is my name--Sergeant Woods. I trust some time, sir, I shall be in a position to return the compliment. Good-evening, sir; God bless your honor! and accept the blessing of an old soldier. And the dear old hero goes down the darken-ing avenue, not so steady of bearing as when he withstood the charge of Pickett on Cemetery Hill, and with the independence of the American citizen who deserves well of his country, makes his way to the nearest hospitable tavern.

THE ISLAND OF BIMINI

To the northward of Hispaniola lies the island of Bimini. It may not be one of the spice islands, but it grows the best ginger to be found in the world. In it is a fair city, and beside the city a lofty mountain, at the foot of which is a noble spring called the 'Fons Juventutis'. This fountain has a sweet savor, as of all manner of spicery, and every hour of the day the water changes its savor and its smell. Whoever drinks of this well will be healed of whatever malady he has, and will seem always young. It is not reported that women and men who drink of this fountain will be always young, but that they will seem so, and probably to themselves, which simply means, in our modern accuracy of language, that they will feel young. This island has never been found. Many voyages have been made in search of it in ships and in the imagination, and Liars have said they have landed on it and drunk of the water, but they never could guide any one else thither. In the credulous centuries when these voyages were made, other islands were discovered, and a continent much more important than Bimini; but these discoveries were a disappointment, because they were not what the adventurers wanted. They did not understand that they had found a new land in which the world should renew its youth and begin a new career. In time the quest was given up, and men regarded it as one of the delusions which came to an end in the sixteenth century. In our day no one has tried to reach Bimini except Heine. Our scientific period has a proper contempt for all such superstitions. We now know that the 'Fons Juventutis' is in every man, and that if actually juvenility cannot be renewed, the advance of age can be arrested and the waste of tissues be prevented, and an uncalculated length of earthly existence be secured, by the injection of some sort of fluid into the system. The right fluid has not yet been discovered by science, but millions of people thought that it had the other day, and now confidently expect it. This credulity has a scientific basis, and has no relation to the old absurd belief in Bimini. We thank goodness that we do not live in a credulous age.

The world would be in a poor case indeed if it had not always before it some ideal or millennial condition, some panacea, some transmutation of base metals into gold, some philosopher's stone, some fountain of youth, some process of turning charcoal into diamonds, some scheme for eliminating evil. But it is worth mentioning that in the historical evolution we have always got better things than we sought or imagined, developments on a much grander scale. History is strewn with the wreck of popular delusions, but always in place of them have come realizations more astonishing than the wildest fancies of the dreamers. Florida was a disappointment as a Bimini, so were the land of the Ohio, the land of the Mississippi, the Dorado of the Pacific coast. But as the illusions, pushed always westward, vanished in the light of common day, lo! a continent gradually emerged, with millions of people animated by conquering ambition of progress in freedom; an industrial continent, covered with a network of steel, heated by steam, and lighted by electricity. What a spectacle of youth on a grand scale is this! Christopher Columbus had not the slightest conception of what he was doing when he touched the button. But we are not satisfied. Quite as far from being so as ever. The popular imagination runs a hard race with any possible natural development. Being in possession of so much, we now expect to travel in the air, to read news in the sending mind before it is sent, to create force without cost, to be transported without time, and to make everybody equal in fortune and happiness to everybody else by act of Congress. Such confidence have we in the power of a "resolution" of the people and by the people that it seems feasible to make women into men, oblivious of the more important and imperative task that will then arise of making men into women. Some of these expectations are only Biminis of the present, but when they have vanished there will be a social and industrial world quite beyond our present conceptions, no doubt. In the article of woman, for instance, she may not become the being that the convention expects, but there may appear a Woman of whom all the Aspasias and Helens were only the faintest types. And although no progress will take the conceit out of men, there may appear a Man so amenable to ordinary reason that he will give up the notion that he can lift himself up by his bootstraps, or make one grain of wheat two by calling it two.

One of the Biminis that have always been looked for is an American Literature. There was an impression that there must be such a thing somewhere on a continent that has everything else. We gave the world tobacco and the potato, perhaps the most important contributions to the content and the fatness of the world made by any new country, and it was a noble ambition to give it new styles of art and literature also. There seems to have been an impression that a literature was something indigenous or ready-made, like any other purely native product, not needing any special period of cultivation or development, and that a nation would be in a mortifying position without one, even before it staked out its cities or built any roads. Captain John Smith, if he had ever settled here and spread himself over the continent, as he was capable of doing, might have taken the contract to furnish one, and we may be sure that he would have left us nothing to desire in that direction. But the vein of romance he opened was not followed up. Other prospectings were made. Holes, so to speak, were dug in New England, and in the middle South, and along the frontier, and such leads were found that again and again the certainty arose that at last the real American ore had been discovered. Meantime a certain process called civilization went on, and certain ideas of breadth entered into our conceptions, and ideas also of the historical development of the expression of thought in the world, and with these a comprehension of what American really is, and the difficulty of putting the contents of a bushel measure into a pint cup. So, while we have been expecting the American Literature to come out from some locality, neat and clean, like a nugget, or, to change the figure, to bloom any day like a century-plant, in one striking, fragrant expression of American life, behold something else has been preparing and maturing, larger and more promising than our early anticipations. In history, in biography, in science, in the essay, in the novel and story, there are coming forth a hundred expressions of the hundred aspects of American life; and they are also sung by the poets in notes as varied as the migrating birds. The birds perhaps have the best of it thus far, but the bird is limited to a small range of performances while he shifts his singing-boughs through the climates of the continent, whereas the poet, though a little inclined to mistake aspiration for inspiration, and vagueness of longing for subtlety, is experimenting in a most hopeful manner. And all these writers, while perhaps not consciously American or consciously seeking to do more than their best in their several ways, are animated by the free spirit of inquiry and expression that belongs to an independent nation, and so our literature is coming to have a stamp of its own that is unlike any other national stamp. And it will have this stamp more authentically and be clearer and stronger as we drop the self-consciousness of the necessity of being American.

JUNE

Here is June again! It never was more welcome in these Northern latitudes. It seems a pity that such a month cannot be twice as long. It has been the pet of the poets, but it is not spoiled, and is just as full of enchantment as ever. The secret of this is that it is the month of both hope and fruition. It is the girl of eighteen, standing with all her charms on the eve of womanhood, in the dress and temperament of spring. And the beauty of it is that almost every woman is young, if ever she were young, in June. For her the roses bloom, and the red clover. It is a pity the month is so short. It is as full of vigor as of beauty. The energy of the year is not yet spent; indeed, the world is opening on all sides; the school-girl is about to graduate into liberty; and the young man is panting to kick or row his way into female adoration and general notoriety. The young men have made no mistake about the kind of education that is popular with women. The women like prowess and the manly virtues of pluck and endurance. The world has not changed in this respect. It was so with the Greeks; it was so when youth rode in tournaments and unhorsed each other for the love of a lady. June is the knightly month. On many a field of gold and green the heroes will kick their way into fame; and bands of young women, in white, with their diplomas in their hands, star-eyed mathematicians and linguists, will come out to smile upon the victors in that exhibition of strength that women most admire. No, the world is not decaying or losing its juvenility. The motto still is, "Love, and may the best man win!" How jocund and immortal is woman! Now, in a hundred schools and colleges, will stand up the solemn, well-intentioned man before a row of pretty girls, and tell them about Womanhood and its Duties, and they will listen just as shyly as if they were getting news, and needed to be instructed by a man on a subject which has engaged their entire attention since they were five years old. In the light of science and experience the conceit of men is something curious. And in June! the most blossoming, riant, feminine time of the year. The month itself is a liberal education to him who is not insensible to beauty and the strong sweet promise of life. The streams run clear then, as they do not in April; the sky is high and transparent; the world seems so large and fresh and inviting. Our houses, which six months in the year in these latitudes are fortifications of defense, are open now, and the breath of life flows through them. Even over the city the sky is benign, and all the country is a heavenly exhibition. May was sweet and capricious. This is the maidenhood deliciousness of the year. If you were to bisect the heart of a true poet, you would find written therein JUNE.

www.bookjungle.com *email: sales@bookjungle.com fax: 630-214-0564 mail: Book Jungle PO Box 2226 Champaign, IL 61825*

The Codes Of Hammurabi And Moses
W. W. Davies

QTY

The discovery of the Hammurabi Code is one of the greatest achievements of archaeology, and is of paramount interest, not only to the student of the Bible, but also to all those interested in ancient history...

Religion   **ISBN:** *1-59462-338-4*   **Pages:132**
MSRP $12.95

The Theory of Moral Sentiments
Adam Smith

QTY

This work from 1749. contains original theories of conscience amd moral judgment and it is the foundation for systemof morals.

Philosophy ISBN: *1-59462-777-0*   **Pages:536**
MSRP $19.95

Jessica's First Prayer
Hesba Stretton

QTY

In a screened and secluded corner of one of the many railway-bridges which span the streets of London there could be seen a few years ago, from five o'clock every morning until half past eight, a tidily set-out coffee-stall, consisting of a trestle and board, upon which stood two large tin cans, with a small fire of charcoal burning under each so as to keep the coffee boiling during the early hours of the morning when the work-people were thronging into the city on their way to their daily toil...

Childrens ISBN: *1-59462-373-2*   **Pages:84**
MSRP $9.95

My Life and Work
Henry Ford

QTY

Henry Ford revolutionized the world with his implementation of mass production for the Model T automobile. Gain valuable business insight into his life and work with his own auto-biography... "We have only started on our development of our country we have not as yet, with all our talk of wonderful progress, done more than scratch the surface. The progress has been wonderful enough but..."

Biographies/ ISBN: *1-59462-198-5*   **Pages:300**
MSRP $21.95

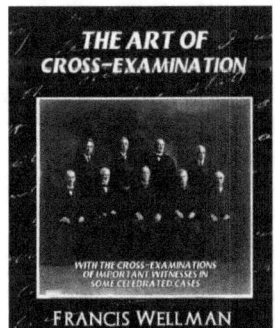

The Art of Cross-Examination
Francis Wellman

QTY

I presume it is the experience of every author, after his first book is published upon an important subject, to be almost overwhelmed with a wealth of ideas and illustrations which could readily have been included in his book, and which to his own mind, at least, seem to make a second edition inevitable. Such certainly was the case with me; and when the first edition had reached its sixth impression in five months, I rejoiced to learn that it seemed to my publishers that the book had met with a sufficiently favorable reception to justify a second and considerably enlarged edition. ..

Pages:412

Reference   ISBN: *1-59462-647-2*   *MSRP $19.95*

On the Duty of Civil Disobedience
Henry David Thoreau

QTY

Thoreau wrote his famous essay, On the Duty of Civil Disobedience, as a protest against an unjust but popular war and the immoral but popular institution of slave-owning. He did more than write—he declined to pay his taxes, and was hauled off to gaol in consequence. Who can say how much this refusal of his hastened the end of the war and of slavery ?

Law   ISBN: *1-59462-747-9*

Pages:48

MSRP $7.45

Dream Psychology Psychoanalysis for Beginners
Sigmund Freud

QTY

Sigmund Freud, born Sigismund Schlomo Freud (May 6, 1856 - September 23, 1939), was a Jewish-Austrian neurologist and psychiatrist who co-founded the psychoanalytic school of psychology. Freud is best known for his theories of the unconscious mind, especially involving the mechanism of repression; his redefinition of sexual desire as mobile and directed towards a wide variety of objects; and his therapeutic techniques, especially his understanding of transference in the therapeutic relationship and the presumed value of dreams as sources of insight into unconscious desires.

Dream Psychology
Psychoanalysis for Beginners

Sigmund Freud

Pages:196

Psychology   ISBN: *1-59462-905-6*   *MSRP $15.45*

The Miracle of Right Thought
Orison Swett Marden

QTY

Believe with all of your heart that you will do what you were made to do. When the mind has once formed the habit of holding cheerful, happy, prosperous pictures, it will not be easy to form the opposite habit. It does not matter how improbable or how far away this realization may see, or how dark the prospects may be, if we visualize them as best we can, as vividly as possible, hold tenaciously to them and vigorously struggle to attain them, they will gradually become actualized, realized in the life. But a desire, a longing without endeavor, a yearning abandoned or held indifferently will vanish without realization.

Pages:360

Self Help   ISBN: *1-59462-644-8*   *MSRP $25.45*

The Rosicrucian Cosmo-Conception Mystic Christianity *by Max Heindel*   ISBN: *1-59462-188-8*   **$38.95**
The Rosicrucian Cosmo-conception is not dogmatic, neither does it appeal to any other authority than the reason of the student. It is: not controversial, but is: sent forth in the, hope that it may help to clear...   New Age/Religion Pages 646

Abandonment To Divine Providence *by Jean-Pierre de Caussade*   ISBN: *1-59462-228-0*   **$25.95**
"The Rev. Jean Pierre de Caussade was one of the most remarkable spiritual writers of the Society of Jesus in France in the 18th Century. His death took place at Toulouse in 1751. His works have gone through many editions and have been republished...   Inspirational/Religion Pages 400

Mental Chemistry *by Charles Haanel*   ISBN: *1-59462-192-6*   **$23.95**
Mental Chemistry allows the change of material conditions by combining and appropriately utilizing the power of the mind. Much like applied chemistry creates something new and unique out of careful combinations of chemicals the mastery of mental chemistry...   New Age Pages 354

The Letters of Robert Browning and Elizabeth Barret Barrett 1845-1846 vol II   ISBN: *1-59462-193-4*   **$35.95**
by Robert Browning and Elizabeth Barrett   Biographies Pages 596

Gleanings In Genesis (volume I) *by Arthur W. Pink*   ISBN: *1-59462-130-6*   **$27.45**
Appropriately has Genesis been termed "the seed plot of the Bible" for in it we have, in germ form, almost all of the great doctrines which are afterwards fully developed in the books of Scripture which follow...   Religion/Inspirational Pages 420

The Master Key *by L. W. de Laurence*   ISBN: *1-59462-001-6*   **$30.95**
In no branch of human knowledge has there been a more lively increase of the spirit of research during the past few years than in the study of Psychology, Concentration and Mental Discipline. The requests for authentic lessons in Thought Control, Mental Discipline and...   New Age/Business Pages 422

The Lesser Key Of Solomon Goetia *by L. W. de Laurence*   ISBN: *1-59462-092-X*   **$9.95**
This translation of the first book of the "Lernegton" which is now for the first time made accessible to students of Talismanic Magic was done, after careful collation and edition, from numerous Ancient Manuscripts in Hebrew, Latin, and French...   New Age/Occult Pages 92

Rubaiyat Of Omar Khayyam *by Edward Fitzgerald*   ISBN:*1-59462-332-5*   **$13.95**
Edward Fitzgerald, whom the world has already learned, in spite of his own efforts to remain within the shadow of anonymity, to look upon as one of the rarest poets of the century, was born at Bredfield, in Suffolk, on the 31st of March, 1809. He was the third son of John Purcell...   Music Pages 172

Ancient Law *by Henry Maine*   ISBN: *1-59462-128-4*   **$29.95**
The chief object of the following pages is to indicate some of the earliest ideas of mankind, as they are reflected in Ancient Law, and to point out the relation of those ideas to modern thought.   Religion/History Pages 452

Far-Away Stories *by William J. Locke*   ISBN: *1-59462-129-2*   **$19.45**
"Good wine needs no bush, but a collection of mixed vintages does. And this book is just such a collection. Some of the stories I do not want to remain buried for ever in the museum files of dead magazine-numbers an author's not unpardonable vanity..."   Fiction Pages 272

Life of David Crockett *by David Crockett*   ISBN: *1-59462-250-7*   **$27.45**
"Colonel David Crockett was one of the most remarkable men of the times in which he lived. Born in humble life, but gifted with a strong will, an indomitable courage, and unremitting perseverance...   Biographies/New Age Pages 424

Lip-Reading *by Edward Nitchie*   ISBN: *1-59462-206-X*   **$25.95**
Edward B. Nitchie, founder of the New York School for the Hard of Hearing, now the Nitchie School of Lip-Reading, Inc, wrote "LIP-READING Principles and Practice". The development and perfecting of this meritorious work on lip-reading was an undertaking...   How-to Pages 400

A Handbook of Suggestive Therapeutics, Applied Hypnotism, Psychic Science   ISBN: *1-59462-214-0*   **$24.95**
by Henry Munro   Health/New Age/Health/Self-help Pages 376

A Doll's House: and Two Other Plays *by Henrik Ibsen*   ISBN: *1-59462-112-8*   **$19.95**
Henrik Ibsen created this classic when in revolutionary 1848 Rome. Introducing some striking concepts in playwriting for the realist genre, this play has been studied the world over.   Fiction/Classics/Plays 308

The Light of Asia *by sir Edwin Arnold*   ISBN: *1-59462-204-3*   **$13.95**
In this poetic masterpiece, Edwin Arnold describes the life and teachings of Buddha. The man who was to become known as Buddha to the world was born as Prince Gautama of India but he rejected the worldly riches and abandoned the reigns of power when...   Religion/History/Biographies Pages 170

The Complete Works of Guy de Maupassant *by Guy de Maupassant*   ISBN: *1-59462-157-8*   **$16.95**
"For days and days, nights and nights, I had dreamed of that first kiss which was to consecrate our engagement, and I knew not on what spot I should put my lips..."   Fiction/Classics Pages 240

The Art of Cross-Examination *by Francis L. Wellman*   ISBN: *1-59462-309-0*   **$26.95**
Written by a renowned trial lawyer, Wellman imparts his experience and uses case studies to explain how to use psychology to extract desired information through questioning.   How-to/Science/Reference Pages 408

Answered or Unanswered? *by Louisa Vaughan*   ISBN: *1-59462-248-5*   **$10.95**
Miracles of Faith in China   Religion Pages 112

The Edinburgh Lectures on Mental Science (1909) *by Thomas*   ISBN: *1-59462-008-3*   **$11.95**
This book contains the substance of a course of lectures recently given by the writer in the Queen Street Hall, Edinburgh. Its purpose is to indicate the Natural Principles governing the relation between Mental Action and Material Conditions...   New Age/Psychology Pages 148

Ayesha *by H. Rider Haggard*   ISBN: *1-59462-301-5*   **$24.95**
Verily and indeed it is the unexpected that happens! Probably if there was one person upon the earth from whom the Editor of this, and of a certain previous history, did not expect to hear again...   Classics Pages 380

Ayala's Angel *by Anthony Trollope*   ISBN: *1-59462-352-X*   **$29.95**
The two girls were both pretty, but Lucy who was twenty-one who supposed to be simple and comparatively unattractive, whereas Ayala was credited, as her Bombwhat romantic name might show, with poetic charm and a taste for romance. Ayala when her father died was nineteen...   Fiction Pages 484

The American Commonwealth *by James Bryce*   ISBN: *1-59462-286-8*   **$34.45**
An interpretation of American democratic political theory. It examines political mechanics and society from the perspective of Scotsman James Bryce   Politics Pages 572

Stories of the Pilgrims *by Margaret P. Pumphrey*   ISBN: *1-59462-116-0*   **$17.95**
This book explores pilgrims religious oppression in England as well as their escape to Holland and eventual crossing to America on the Mayflower, and their early days in New England...   History Pages 268

QTY

The Fasting Cure *by Sinclair Upton*   ISBN: *1-59462-222-1*   **$13.95**
In the Cosmopolitan Magazine for May, 1910, and in the Contemporary Review (London) for April, 1910, I published an article dealing with my experi-ences in fasting. I have written a great many magazine articles, but never one which attracted so much attention... New Age/Self Help/Health Pages 164

Hebrew Astrology *by Sepharial*   ISBN: *1-59462-308-2*   **$13.45**
In these days of advanced thinking it is a matter of common observation that we have left many of the old landmarks behind and that we are now pressing forward to greater heights and to a wider horizon than that which represented the mind-content of our progenitors...   Astrology Pages 144

Thought Vibration or The Law of Attraction in the Thought World   ISBN: *1-59462-127-6*   **$12.95**
by William Walker Atkinson   *Psychology/Religion Pages 144*

Optimism *by Helen Keller*   ISBN: *1-59462-108-X*   **$15.95**
Helen Keller was blind, deaf, and mute since 19 months old, yet famously learned how to overcome these handicaps, communicate with the world, and spread her lectures promoting optimism. An inspiring read for everyone...   Biographies/Inspirational Pages 84

Sara Crewe *by Frances Burnett*   ISBN: *1-59462-360-0*   **$9.45**
In the first place, Miss Minchin lived in London. Her home was a large, dull, tall one, in a large, dull square, where all the houses were alike, and all the sparrows were alike, and where all the door-knockers made the same heavy sound...   Childrens/Classic Pages 88

The Autobiography of Benjamin Franklin *by Benjamin Franklin*   ISBN: *1-59462-135-7*   **$24.95**
The Autobiography of Benjamin Franklin has probably been more extensively read than any other American historical work, and no other book of its kind has had such ups and downs of fortune. Franklin lived for many years in England, where he was agent...   Biographies/History Pages 332

Name	
Email	
Telephone	
Address	
City, State ZIP	

☐ **Credit Card**   ☐ **Check / Money Order**

Credit Card Number	
Expiration Date	
Signature	

Please Mail to: Book Jungle
PO Box 2226
Champaign, IL 61825
or Fax to: 630-214-0564

ORDERING INFORMATION

web*: www.bookjungle.com*
email*: sales@bookjungle.com*
fax*: 630-214-0564*
mail*: Book Jungle PO Box 2226 Champaign, IL 61825*
or PayPal *to sales@bookjungle.com*

Please contact us for bulk discounts

DIRECT-ORDER TERMS

20% Discount if You Order Two or More Books
Free Domestic Shipping!
Accepted: Master Card, Visa,
Discover, American Express

www.ingramcontent.com/pod-product-compliance
Lightning Source LLC
Chambersburg PA
CBHW082016170626
46817CB00009B/3118